THE BRIBE

of

Great Price

BART PIERCE

The Bribe of Great Price

BART PIERCE

The Bribe of Great Price

ISBN 10: 0970475357
ISBN 13: 9780970475350

Printed in the United States of America.
All rights reserved under International Copyright Law.
Copyright 2007 by Bart Pierce

ALL RIGHTS RESERVED

Published by:
GateKeeper Publishing, LLC.
P.O. Box 0344
Cheshire, CT. 06410

www.gatekeeperpublishing.com

Cover design by April Campbell
GateKeeper Publishing, LLC.

Library of Congress Cataloging-in-Publication Data
Pierce, Bart

The Bribe of Great Price

ISBN 978-09704753-5-0 (Paper-back)
1. Christian Living • Church Ministry

Endorsements for
THE BRIBE OF GREAT PRICE

Bishop Bart Pierce has done the Church World a favor. He has exposed the diabolical plans of Satan through "The Bribe", to keep the Church from being the powerful, militant people of God who refuse to compromise or be seduced by satan's bribe.

This book will flame the righteous fiery zeal of God within you. It will stir the "Mighty Man of War" within to arise and demonstrate the resurrected living Christ. This book needs to be read by every Christian who wants to be mightily used of God to demonstrate Christ's power in mighty miracles, financial prosperity and uncompromising demonstration that Jesus is the only way, the only truth and the only life for mankind.

— Dr. Bill Hamon
Bishop of Christian International Ministries Network (CIMN)
Author of "Day of The Saints"

"The Bribe is a wakeup call to the Body of Christ. Bishop Pierce has unveiled the current deceptions that have contributed to the current state of the Church and its failure to influence culture. A helpful resource for anyone wanting to better understand where we are and what we must do to reclaim our culture for Jesus Christ."

Os Hillman
Author of TGIF: Today God is First
President of Marketplace Leaders

Bart Pierce is a man of great courage who exposes a shocking truth! The Bribe touches every area of society and exposes the secret sell-out by the power brokers in religious, governmental, and economic circles. Lies, cover ups, and conspiracies are revealed in The Bribe to keep many from the knowledge of the greatest truth. The Bribe is a must read for everyone.

Dr. John P. Kelly
CEO, ICWBF (International Christian WealthBuilders Foundation)
Founder/President, LEAD (Leadership Education for Apostolic Development)
Founder/Ambassador, ICA (International Coalition of Apostles)

Bishop Bart Pierce is clearly a voice to the church of today. As many of us follow God's leading, into Marketplace Ministry, and wealth creation, there is great need for "grounding". Bishop Bart Pierce's life and ministry are proof that you can succeed in ministry and business simultaneously. Who better to remind us of the need for balance? For those of us who minister to the business community, teaching Christians the Biblical principles for wealth creation, there is a very clear danger, of allowing wealth and success to eclipse the central message of the Bible – the death, burial and resurrection of our Lord & Savior, Jesus Christ. I like the fact that Bart not only identifies the problems within our culture and society, but also offers definitive solutions which each of us can implement in our lives and ministries. The Bribe is a timely reminder to all of us, that if our ministry or our integrity can be bought, the enemy stands ready to meet our price – to bribe us to sell out for that which pales in comparison to our Savior.

Thank you, Bishop Bart, for reminding us of the one true central message of Christianity. May we never sell out to the Bribe!

Mark Gorman,
Minister & Motivational Speaker
Author of God's Plan For Prosperity

Table of Contents

INTRODUCTION

"In the last days perilous times will come," Paul writes in 2 Timothy 3:1. (NKJV)

We are living in such times. Corruption is out of control, war drums are rumbling louder and louder, and churches seem less and less willing to step up and address critical issues. Is it that the Church, like our government and our school systems, has turned her face from the reality of the issues at hand?

Have we, like Hollywood and Wall Street, reached under the table of compromise and denial and taken The Bribe, like the soldiers did in Matthew 28? Two thousand years ago, the religious leaders and the elders of the city of Jerusalem offered them the bribe to keep them quiet and to make sure that the word never got out that Jesus is alive and that He did conquer death, hell and the grave.

THE ANTE IS RAISED

This Bribe has been paid out for 2000 years and the ante has gone up. It keeps getting more costly ever day. Now, Hollywood is willing to invest billions of dollars to produce movies like "The Da Vinci Code" (and others) that are designed to silence the voice of His Church. The politicians are working night and day to pass laws that outlaw God from our schools, our government, our homes, and our money.

The Bribe amount is reaching all time highs, mounting up until America—One Nation Under God—is only a faint memory of a compromised past, to the point that our professors are convinced that man is the ultimate creator and the planet can be destroyed by man because there's no god who can intercede or stop man from doing whatever he wants.

Bribe is the right word to describe and expose the hideous plan of Satan to keep the Word buried, to stop the truth from breaking out, to keep Christ's Church from paying whatever it costs and sacrificing whatever it takes to make sure that 2000 years of paid-off silence will end now.

This book is a prophetic story, a challenge to stop taking Hollywood, Wall Street, and the political bribe to keep the Church silent. Now is the time to shout, to invest, and to pay whatever it costs to see the Gospel of the Kingdom go forth loud and clear!

Chapter One

The Plot of plots

After 2,000 years, the bribe is still being paid.

Matthew describes what happened 20 centuries ago:

> Now while they were on their way, some of
> the guard came into the city and reported
> to the chief priests all that had happened.
> And when they had assembled with the
> elders and consulted together, they gave
> a large sum of money to the soldiers, and
> said, "You are to say, 'His disciples came

by night and stole Him away while we were asleep.' "And if this should come to the governor's ears, we will win him over and keep you out of trouble." And they took the money and did as they had been instructed; and this story was widely spread among the Jews, and is to this day.

—MATTHEW 28:11-15 NASU

The guards who knew the truth were being paid to communicate a falsehood. Twenty centuries later, this bribery deal is still being struck in the dark rooms and corners of society's establishment.

This IS the original bribe, paid to COVER a lie.

The chief priests represented the elitist core that dominates and controls the information and thought of a culture. Today, in most nations, the establishment consists of information, education and governing elites. Many of them still pay the bribe to cover the truth that Christ is alive.

Imagine the scene 2,000 years ago, and you get a feel for what is happening now. The Roman soldiers who had been guarding Christ's tomb wake up from a strange sleep, and discover the grave is empty. What do they do? If they report the vacant tomb to their superiors, they might get punished. Worse, if they don't tell their leaders, and word comes by someone else, they may be killed. If they go AWOL, they will surely be caught, and die in humiliation as traitors to Rome.

WHY DID THEY LEAVE THEIR POST?

For centuries, people who wanted to disprove Christ's Resurrection have tried to explain why those Roman guards left their duty at the tomb. Roman soldiers worried about the smallest details of their work because they knew what would happen if they failed.

One way they were punished was being burned alive with their own robes. One man who studied the way the Romans disciplined their soldiers wrote that the fear of horrible punishment "produced flawless attention to duty, especially in the night watches." [1]

You can envision the story they probably told.

Reluctantly, they decide to report. But to whom do they give their shocking story? Pilate, Caesar's representative, will lop off their heads for falling asleep on the job. Pilate had washed his hands of any complicity in Jesus' crucifixion, and he would just as well try to distance himself from any suggestion of Christ's resurrection. The soldiers decide to go to the high priest and his council, the Sanhedrin. This Christ-business was their problem anyway.

"We were at the tomb, and something really weird happened. That guy you beat up, the one we Romans mocked as the 'King of the Jews'— you know, the one you tore up and whose clothes we gambled over, the criminal whose head we crowned with thorns and did everything possible to get rid of is no longer in the tomb! You're probably not going to believe this, but there we were, alert and on the job, with our swords, spears and shields in place. We were like that all night. Then suddenly men we'd never seen appeared out of nowhere. They weren't normal people. Their faces glowed like lightning, and we could barely look at them. Their presence paralyzed us. Our eyes were open, but our minds were dumbfounded."

they Must devise a plan to Hide the fact that Jesus was indeed the Messiah.

The religious establishment is deeply troubled. They know the soldiers chosen for the strategic mission of guarding Jesus' tomb are the cream of the Roman crop. They are men of reputation, who wouldn't lie. The religious power-brokers remember Jesus' said He would come back. Now they know they must devise a plan to hide the fact that Jesus was indeed the genuine Messiah.

Centuries earlier, Moses had sent 12 spies to check out the Promised Land Israel was preparing to enter after 400 years of slavery in Egypt and 40 years of wandering in the wilderness. They came back with reports of a land overflowing with abundance, but with a troubling problem—there were fierce giants there. Only two of the spies—Joshua and Caleb—were confident Israel could overcome. The other 10 were convinced the cause was hopeless, and Numbers 13:32 says they gave a "bad report."

THE ULTIMATE BAD REPORT

Now, in another age, the ultimate *bad report* is being devised. And the spirit of the "bad report," financed by the bribe, is still with us. In fact, that original bribe, paid to conceal the truth about Jesus Christ, has increased through time. The lie, passed from generation to generation, is ever more costly, because people are smarter.

Hollywood has paid, Wall Street has shelled out, and politicians have spent much to maintain the bribe. They have to keep creating new ways to keep the falsehood alive, to keep the lie going.

the Lie is ever more Costly, because people are smarter.

One example was the attempt by movie producer James Cameron to bribe the public with the idea that the tomb of Jesus and His family had been found in Jerusalem. Cameron dusted off an old, already-disproved archaeological site, and made a television special about it.

But he gave away his motive when he said, "I see our potential destruction and the potential salvation as human beings coming from technology and how we use it, how we master it and how we prevent it from mastering us."

The actual truth is:

- Had there been a "family tomb" containing the remains of Jesus, especially one as prominent as Cameron is hyping, the enemies of Jesus would have used it to quiet all the resurrection talk that continued for decades.

- As a blogger notes, James, Jesus' half-brother, could have averted his bloody martyrdom simply by taking people to the tomb.

- That goes for all the other disciples who died for bearing witness to Christ and His resurrection.

- Historians of the period—like Eusebius—don't mention the family tomb of Jesus, even though it would have been a prominent site in Jerusalem, if for no other reason than to bury the resurrection story forever.

Two thousand years ago, the religious establishment concluded they had to keep people in the dark, and had to prevent them from knowing Jesus rose from the dead, confirming He really was the Messiah. The same desperation drives the lie today, and the bribery that sustains it.

But I am here, like hosts of others, to declare that not even Hollywood, with its immense power of delusion, and its vast wealth, doesn't have enough creativity or money to make the story of Jesus and His resurrection untrue.

I was a drug addict, on my way to Hell. One day the shining glory of God, in the name of Jesus, pierced my life. He lifted me from a filthy pit and placed me on my solid rock. He anchored me there to stay and to stand.

A man with an experience is never at the mercy of a man with a mere argument. So I write this book to uncover this plot of plots, this bribe-fed scheme to cover up who Jesus really is.

I write this book to uncover this Plot of plots, this bribe-fed scheme to cover up who Jesus really Is.

Chapter 2

Paid
everywhere

"If they preach we will take necessary actions under the relevant provision of the law."

The document, issued by the Inspector of Police in a certain city in India, couldn't have been plainer. It named my associates and me, and warned us and our Indian hosts that if we proclaimed God's Word we would be arrested.

We found out about the document when we arrived at the outdoor location where we were to conduct a service. It had been issued while we were in flight. Now we watched as the crowds packed the location for the outdoor camp meeting.

Our arrival in the Indian city had been pleasant. Some 20 pastors met us at the airport, and draped beautiful leis of fresh flowers around our necks.

But when we arrived at the place we were scheduled to preach, not only did we discover the document warning of our arrest, but that the police station was right next door!

I'm not easily intimidated, so I decided I would preach anyway. Our host pastor was frightened. However, we arranged for all four members of our team to speak. When we arrived back at the house where we were staying, the police soon showed up. We refused to go out to meet the chief officer, and demanded he come in to confront us face to face.

I told the policeman I wouldn't accept a verbal warning, and wanted to see the legal document, which he brought to me.

"Sir, you must explain this law to us," I said to the officer.

"We got a report from a Hindu extremist and we're afraid they'll try to bomb this meeting," he replied. Several people, including pastors, have been killed."

One of our team members was an African-American who is a Baltimore police officer. "I'm a lieutenant in a police department," he told the Indian policeman. "Do you mean to tell me you're thinking of arresting me? Is that the consequence if we preach?"

"I'll take your passports and arrest you," the Indian responded.

"Your problem is that you're taking money under the table," I told the policeman. This angered him. "What are you going to do about that?" I asked.

The Indian stormed out of the house. Our four team members sat there, with the pastor and his three young-adult sons.

"Let's go preach," I said. "You don't have to go if you don't want to. When they take me, just call my wife, and tell people where I am."

"If you preach, we'll slap the first policeman who tries to arrest you, and we'll all go to jail together," replied one of the team members.

The Indian pastor hung his head low. I knew instantly the man was fearful. Even though his father had planted more than 2,000 churches, he apparently didn't believe the kind of Gospel we preached.

"Dad, Bishop Pierce is right," said one of the sons of the pastor. "We should go log our complaint, and at least they'd have another opinion."

"I don't know," said another son, as he placed his hand on his father's shoulder.

"Bishop, I can't let you do it," the pastor said.

By now it was four in the morning. We'd driven five hours to get to the town after an even longer flight half way around the world. But we couldn't give up.

"Brother," I said to the pastor, "let's prove something. Get the pastors together in the morning at the church, and I'll speak to them."

When we got to the meeting, the police were there. "You can speak to the pastors, but you can't use a microphone, because we want no amplification outside," an officer said.

I'm all for obeying the law except when the law tells me God is not allowed.

"Sir, you're not going to tell me what I can and can't do in God's house," I replied. We went ahead and used microphones so everyone in the neighborhood could hear. The pastors began shouting and crying, and God moved powerfully.

When we finished the police were nowhere in sight.

I turned to the pastor, "If you let us preach every night we'll see awesome miracles and breakthroughs," I told him.

"I can't allow it," he said. "We need to obey the law."

"I'm all for obeying the law except when the law tells me God is not allowed, then at that point my God and the law of His Kingdom trumps your god and kingdom."

The Indian pastors were still fearful, so our team jumped into a car, headed to the airport, changed our flights and returned home.

Today, the bribe is paid everywhere, in the prevailing currency, but surrender is never an option. That's why I wouldn't yield to the Indian policeman. It's sad that in this generation there are people so paralyzed by fear that the slightest pressure causes them to deny Jesus.

Pastor Barboza, a greatly anointed prophetic man, told the Indian pastor, "Your children will inherit this and they will suffer. Now that the Hindu has taken away your ability for strangers to preach, they will come next and keep you from preaching. The same is true with the radical Muslims."

The reason people like the Indian officials don't want the Gospel preached is desperation in the elites to keep people in the dark about Christ's Resurrection, which proves He is the promised Messiah. In Iran, for example, the Islamic officials are concerned about the growth of the church. [1]

In that country, according to Voice of the Martyrs ministry,

> "Christians are not allowed to print literature, including Sunday bulletins, and converts from Islam to Christianity are labeled apostate and subject to the death penalty. Christian pastors are under constant surveillance, and many are forced to sign documents saying they will not allow Muslims to be in their worship services."[2]

The determination in Iran to keep the bribe going means even the sanctity of the home is violated. "This new wave of persecution is coming against Christians that meet to worship God in the privacy of their homes." according to VOM sources.

"We have confirmed reports that several believers have been interrogated and one house was stormed by an elite police team that confiscated a computer, several CDs and Christian materials. A Christian was arrested in this attack, and remains in prison."

"Clearly, Iran's government is alarmed at the growth of the Christian faith there," said Todd Nettleton, a VOM spokesman.[3] "This is a key time for the church in Iran. We call on Iran's government to release this Christian believer who is being held, and we call on Christians around the world to pray for our brothers and sisters in Iran," he said.

MARTYRED FOR NOT BEING BRIBED

Hindu-dominated governments in several states in India are doing everything possible to keep their people under the influence of the bribe. One pastor left his native Kerala State in the south—where there are many Christians—to become a missionary to India's north. He was beaten and stabbed, but recovered, and founded a Bible school. At least two graduates have been martyred after they went back to their native regions to plant churches and to keep them from telling the truth.

In Afghanistan, lives are threatened to keep people silent, because they have chosen to follow Christ. In Indonesia, two young female followers of Christ are slaughtered in a forest on a walk home, simply because they have embraced the truth that Jesus is alive and is indeed the Messiah. In the Sudan, whole populations are being wiped out because of their commitment to the risen Christ.

And in America and other "sophisticated" western nations, those who know Jesus is alive and is the Son of God are pushed to the edge of the culture, kept from view and finally silenced by those who pay the bribe to keep people from the truth.

Yet the stunning fact stands across time—Jesus Christ is alive! No other religion makes such a claim for its founder. Buddha was alive once, and then he died, as was Mohammed, Confucius and all the rest.

Jesus Christ IS alive! no other religion makes such a claim for its founder.

My wife and I have stood in the tomb in which Jesus is said to have been placed those three days. The barren little cave is an interesting place—because of its emptiness.

No one has been able to refute the reports of Scripture, neither those who lived when Matthew and the other Gospel writers were penning their accounts, nor those who have followed in history. Consider what Matthew tells us:

> Now after the Sabbath, as it began to dawn toward the first day of the week, Mary Magdalene and the other Mary came to look at the grave. And behold, a severe earthquake had occurred, for an angel of the Lord descended from heaven and came and rolled away the stone and sat upon it. And his appearance was like lightning, and his clothing as white as snow. The guards shook for fear of him and became like dead men.
>
> —MATTHEW 28:1-4 NASU

This sounds like something right out of a Stephen Spielberg movie. Here are these tough, even brutal, military professionals standing on knocking knees, paralyzed with fear. Imagine the brightness of a lightning flash. Rather than a split-second appearance, that searing brightness stands in front of them. Matthew continues the report:

The angel said to the women, "Do not be afraid; for I know that you are looking for Jesus who has been crucified. He is not here, for He has risen, just as He said. Come, see the place where He was lying. "Go quickly and tell His disciples that He has risen from the dead; and behold, He is going ahead of you into Galilee, there you will see Him; behold, I have told you." And they left the tomb quickly with fear and great joy and ran to report it to His disciples. (Matthew 28:5-8 NASU)

How could anyone forget such a moment? Think about what those Roman guards must have told their grandchildren! Decades later, how would they have described the brilliant being who stood before them, and the angel-voice? Certainly the women who came to the tomb that morning would carry the memory for the rest of their lives. They would be transformed through the awe-inspiring encounter with the living Christ.

And if the disciples had moved Jesus' body, they would have known what they had done. His followers wouldn't have risked their lives and fortunes to tell the world about Jesus and His resurrection if they knew down deep inside that it hadn't happened.

One time in Uruguay a student asked Josh McDowell—author of many books defending the truth about Christ—why he couldn't refute Christianity. "For a very simple reason," Josh answered. "I am not able to explain away an event in history—the resurrection of Jesus Christ." [4]

THE TRUTH THE BRIBE HIDES

McDowell quotes the famous biblical scholar, F.F. Bruce, who put it like this: "Had there been any tendency to depart from the facts in any material respect, the possible presence of hostile witnesses in the audience would have served as a further corrective." [5]

Then, says Josh McDowell,

> "The most telling testimony of all must be the lives of those early Christians. We must ask ourselves: What caused them to go everywhere telling the message of the risen Christ? Had there been any visible benefits accrued to them from their efforts—prestige, wealth, increased social status or material benefits—we might logically attempt to account for their actions, for their whole-hearted and total allegiance to this "risen Christ." As a reward for their efforts, however, those early Christians were beaten, stoned to death, thrown to the lions, tortured

and crucified. Every conceivable method was used to stop them from talking. Yet, they laid down their lives as the ultimate proof of their complete confidence in the truth of their message." [6]

Maybe the most spectacular moment of all for the women who visited the tomb is recorded by Matthew:

> And as they went to tell His disciples, behold, Jesus met them, saying, "Rejoice!" So they came and held Him by the feet and worshiped Him. Then Jesus said to them, "Do not be afraid. Go and tell My brethren to go to Galilee, and there they will see Me."
>
> —MATTHEW 28:9-10 NKJV

"Rejoice" is the first word from the mouth of the risen Jesus! In the original New Testament Greek, it means to jump up, and spin around in a circle. An incredible thing has happened, and the only way people could respond was with cheering, leaping, dancing joy.

This is among the reasons it's so sad to think about what's happening in our day. Rather than rejoicing, there's a desperate effort to keep the truth from being known. There is a seductive plot going forward today in America and throughout the world.

Rather **than** rejoicing, there's a **desperate** effort **to** keep the **truth** from being **known.**

In my lifetime, I have seen a change, even among some who profess Christ.

In fact, there has never been a time— even before I became a Christian—that I have seen a situation like exists today. All this wickedness is in the context of the One Who rose from the dead. At Christmas, people protest everything from the Christmas tree to the public display of the manger scene. It seems many department stores and other retail establishments crumbled first. It was as if they said they wanted nothing to do with this "baby Jesus," except to take the money flowing around His birthday celebration.

HAPPY HOLIDAYS

Many stores, for example, decided to try to avoid offending customers at Christmas, so they ordered their employees to say to shoppers, "Happy holidays," instead of "Merry Christmas." However, many retailers changed back to the traditional greeting when they found, as a CNN/USA Today Gallup Poll reported, that 69 percent of Americans preferred "Merry Christmas." [7]

Easter, in the non-believing world has become, not a season

to celebrate history's most stunning event, but pagan worship. So Christmas and Easter, in the minds of many, have become mere "holidays," as politically correct seasonal greeting cards put it.

In such a time the words of the prophet Hosea ring with piercing clarity:

Listen to the word of the LORD, O sons of Israel, For the LORD has a case against the inhabitants of the land, because there is no faithfulness or kindness. Or knowledge of God in the land. There is swearing, deception, murder, stealing and adultery. They employ violence, so that bloodshed follows bloodshed ... My people are destroyed for lack of knowledge ... (Hosea 4:1-2, 6)

Throughout America there is a massive effort by media to remove even the simple utterance of the name of Jesus—except as a swear word. In fact, our culture has turned unbelief into an art form. The establishment has recognized some of the perversions, providing government funding for artists depicting Christ in extreme forms of blasphemous works.

In the United Kingdom a group called Breakout Trust raised thousands of dollars to produce a children's film about Jesus, to be used in schools. Steve Legg, creator of the movie, said he took on the project after he heard about a child who, when told about the Nativity, asked his parents why Mary and Joseph would name the Child after a "swear word"! [9]

"There are over 12 million children in the UK and only 756,000 of them go to church regularly. That leaves a staggering number who don't and are probably not receiving basic Christian teaching," Legg said. [10]

> Most Americans say they believe in God, the problem is too few believe God!

Most Americans say they believe in God, according to numerous polls. The problem is too few believe God. If you press the issue of biblical authority with many individuals, they will respond that they are uncertain because, after all, "the Bible was written by men." Unbelieving people often demand that the Bible meet the narrow limits of human intellect and reason. They are actually inferring that the human mind is greater than God, since His revelation must meet its criteria for understanding.

No wonder the Bible says, "The fool has said in his heart, 'there is no God'" (Psalm 14:1; 53:1). How can a fool educate someone who has been with God?

TEACHING UNBELIEF

A young man in our church told me of a religion class he took at the University of Maryland. For six weeks, the lectures focused on the idea that the Bible is not the authentic word of

God, and only two weeks were actually spent on content.

At Temple University, a student was involuntarily committed to a psychiatric institution when he complained about a campus play depicting Jesus as a homosexual.

The cultural establishment, consisting of secular universities like Temple (and sometimes even "Christian" schools), politicians, news media and Hollywood are on a crusade to get rid of the One who rose from the grave.

The Bible has been edited by some to get rid of portions with which there is disagreement, or that don't fit the standards of political correctness and subjective experience.

This practice goes all the way back to Thomas Jefferson. Though he made extremely important contributions to the founding of America, Jefferson made the mistake of trying to edit the Bible. He believed Jesus' ethical teachings were the greatest in history. However, Jefferson was uncomfortable with doctrine and the supernatural, so he sliced out those sections so he could have a Bible that fit his tastes.

Now there's even a seminar of "scholars" who meet annually to decide which Biblical teachings of Jesus are real and which are not.

Many people have been empowered by the spirit of science and technology but rejected the Spirit of God. In fact, as one Christian leader suggested, for many secular people today technology has become modern man's Holy Spirit. They try to use human concepts and techniques to make the Bible say what they want it to say.

This is not new. The bribe was paid initially 2,000 years ago, and has grown exponentially through the centuries. It is still being paid, and the amount is enormous.

Chapter 3

C the urrency of the bribe

The bribe is paid in a variety of currencies. Before Europe had the Euro it had the pound, the frank, the mark, the shilling and other money-types, all pulled into one form—the Euro.

But that's not the adversary's approach. He'll pay individuals and groups in whatever currency they desire—as long as they agree not to believe in the resurrection of Jesus Christ.

Some are most tempted to accept the bribe if it comes in money itself. Like the soldiers at the empty tomb, they like to hear the clank of coins and crinkle of bills.

SUBTLE PRESSURE

For example, let's say a professor at a state university decides to take Christ seriously. She begins to talk openly about the authority of the Bible, and the importance of being transformed by Jesus Christ. The teacher tells her students there might be some questions about Darwinism, the sexual revolution, and other hot-button issues of the day.

> The unbelieving culture tries to bribe people to drop their faith in favor of personal gain.

Soon the professor is called to the academic dean's office. She has tenure, so she can't be fired. However, the academic dean hints that he is thinking of making her head of her department. He tells her, however, that all her Christ-talk has to be muted if she wants the title and big bucks that go with it.

That scenario is played out a thousand times a day as the unbelieving culture tries to bribe people to drop their faith in favor of personal gain.

Another currency in which the bribe is paid is "acceptance." Social groups are the primary pushers of this form of payment.

A kid in one of the classes taught by the professor I described above takes her teacher seriously and accepts Jesus Christ as her Savior and Lord. Word leaks out that the coed has "whacked out" over Christianity and when it comes time for the sorority rush, the young woman—who was a senior favorite in high school—is ignored.

When she asks why she's getting the run-around, she discovers that if she wants to be accepted in a sorority she better ease off this Christian-thing.

Another form of currency for paying the bribe is closely linked to acceptance. It's called "reputation." A guy named George was a top salesman for his company. He outperformed everyone in his region.

However, George discovered he was left out of some of the sales meetings. He later discovered that the meetings were a cover for wild parties. His reputation as a believer excluded him.

"You can either be known as a guy who likes to have a good time or as a guy who's serious about being a Christian, but you can't have both," an associate told him.

It was tempting to compromise since key clients and prospects were invited to the "sales meetings." All George had to do was compromise his reputation, and he would have access to the potential business represented by those clients.

George refused to take the bribe, remained a firm believer in Jesus Christ and His Resurrection, and trusted the Lord for the rest.

THE HARDEST CURRENCIES

The hardest currencies of all are threats, terror and martyrdom. These forms of the bribe are being paid out daily, throughout the world.

In the ancient city of Bethlehem, for example, there was once a thriving community of Arab Christians, but as Islam muscled its way in, many of the Christians had to flee for their lives. Now Christians in Christ's birthplace are a virtual minority, increasingly isolated from their own community because of threats, terror, and even martyrdom.

Faith McDonnell writes:

> Since gaining independence in 1956, Sudan has been plagued by civil war, the result of the Sudanese government's desire to Islamize and Arabize all of Sudan. This so-called "Sudanization" of Sudan disregards the "Africa-ness" of much of the country: the multiplicity of languages and dialects, the Sudanese with black skin, the traditional religions of the Nilotic region, and the Christian identity of Sudan that reaches back beyond the Christians of

southern Sudan, beyond the ancient Christian kingdoms of Nubia, beyond the conversion of the court official of Queen Candace of Meroe, to the prophecies of Isaiah 18, Ezekiel 29, and Zephaniah 2.

When interviewed by the Episcopal News Service in 1999, southern Sudanese politician and human rights lawyer Abel Alier spelled out the intentions of the current regime. "The Sudanese government is on an Islamic crusade," he said, explaining that it has long been the agenda of radical Islamists to see if a country of varied racial, cultural, and religious populations could be totally Islamized and Arabized. The "Sudanese experiment," well-funded by the Arab world, would be followed by the rest of Africa, and beyond. [1]

The global Islamic terrorist movement is doling out hefty amounts of the bribes of threat, terror and martyrdom to make sure people don't accept the fact of Christ's Resurrection.

THE BRIBE AND THE POVERTY ATTITUDE

Many churches in affluent societies fall to the lure of the bribe because, though they exist in the middle of a lot of wealth, they have a poverty mentality. They have bought into

> **Many** churches **in affluent** societies fall **lure** to the **bribe** because they **have** a **poverty** mentality.

the idea that poverty means piety and holiness. Actually that lie came in with the bribe, and is part of the enemy's plan for keeping the church from being successful, advancing the Kingdom of God, and living above the adversary and his schemes rather than beneath.

The use of money is among the greatest principles of the Kingdom of God. Giving is mentioned more than 4,000 times in the Bible. The foundation of the principle is found in the words of John 3:16, "God so loved the world that He gave..."

When I walked into the Kingdom upon being saved in the 1970s, the Kingdom principles about finance and money were among the first I learned. I put the principles into practice. We had money from drug deals and from silver wedding gifts, and gave it all to the church. This act opened a revelation that gave me understanding of the rest of the Bible. Giving away that money unlocked something in my heart!

If you put into practice the truths the Bible reveals about finance and money, your finances will change within six months to a year. I've experienced this myself.

And when that happens, the bribe loses its appeal.

We need to set aside bad thinking and renew our minds with fresh information. This will break off the old habits and the lies of the Bribe that have been passed down through the ages. We will discover the wonderful fact that God promised us the power to get wealth for the purpose of advancing His Kingdom.

Victory is the defeat of an enemy, of triumphing over something or someone. That's where we are today, taking the steps that lead us to a different place financially.

Our adversary has succeeded in keeping the truth about God's plan for prosperity quiet. He's hushed the message of wealth and victory and financial blessing, and he's used hush money to do it! Then the evil one has hoarded all the wealth for himself and the invasions of his dark kingdom, all across the ages. The success in your struggle against difficulties and obstacles comes when you wake up to what's been taken from you and take positive steps to get it back. We have to become as shrewd and discerning as Paul, who wrote that Satan can't take advantage of us when we're aware of his schemes. (2 Corinthians 2:12)

One of these schemes is giving churches a "non-profit" self-image. The truth is that nothing about God is non-profit! He intended every facet of life to be profitable. The natural world reveals this as well as the Bible, in that life begets life, and there is bounty and blessing throughout the natural order because of

THE *Bribe* of Great Price •

the laws God has placed into the universe. Yet, many churches do not walk in this truth.

There's no temptation to take currency when you experience God's provision. I'm amazed daily at the money that comes my way. One day at church I gave money to a person in need, walked across the room and somebody gave me money before I could get on the platform. God is able to take care of me. Why would I need a bribe?

LIBERATION!

It's a joy not to be bound to money. It's like a yoke of slavery is taken off your neck. Obedience to God's Word, coupled with diligence and hard work set us free!

> Some people have been in poverty so long they'er proud of being poor.

This liberty brought by God comes in the form of a brand new attitude. Some people have been in poverty so long they're proud of being poor. But it's not God's plan for people to be poor and impoverished. In Haiti, the poorest nation in the Western Hemisphere, I challenged 1,000 people in a conference to give. My wife and I modeled the message by giving away whatever we had available, on the spot.

The people in the audience began doing the same. I watched a man give away a stalk of bananas, and another a calf. Month's later precious fresh water was found on the very land where the giving took place. Not only was new, fresh water found, it was of a higher quality than water in many other parts of Haiti.

The ministry in that region exploded. The people who lived by God's Word discovered that their prosperity wasn't dependent on the nation's economic condition. They lived in the Kingdom of God, even though physically they were in a poor society.

Those Haitians were freed from a poverty attitude. For me that means there's not a day when I walk around talking about what I don't have. I delight in what I do have, and I worship, praise and thank God for it.

Liberation comes as we act on the principle of tithing.

The liberation comes as we act on the principle of tithing. And that means actually doing it. We have to stop saying we can't tithe. It's not really a choice, but God's command. As we are obedient, we learn that we can give our way out of debt.

The next step to freedom is to increase your offering weekly, even if it's only by 10-cents. If you have to reduce your intake to increase your outflow, I advise you to do it. You'll begin to see the blessing of God. That's what He said through Malachi:

"Bring the whole tithe into the storehouse, so that there may be food in My house, and test Me now in this," says the LORD of hosts, "if I will not open for you the windows of heaven and pour out for you a blessing until it overflows. Then I will rebuke the devourer for you, so that it will not destroy the fruits of the ground; nor will your vine in the field cast its grapes," says the LORD of hosts. All the nations will call you blessed, for you shall be a delightful land," says the LORD of hosts."

—MALACHI 3:1-11

The tithe is a "devoted thing," marked for destruction or consumption. Give it to God and it will be used to destroy the destroyer. If you steal and hoard it, it'll destroy you. Remember Achan? He defied God's command that all the spoil of Jericho be dedicated to Him, and took a Babylonian garment and some other treasures, hiding them in his tent (see Joshua 7). Achan's act of taking what had been devoted to God destroyed him and his family.

Adam and Eve, ate the fruit, which was a "devoted thing" to God, and which they weren't to touch, and they lost Paradise and opened the gates of the world to sin and death.

The bounty of God comes from an open Heaven, but when we take what is God's, "thy heaven that is over thy head

shall be brass, and the earth that is under thee shall be iron."
(Deuteronomy 28:23)

That condition, brought about by disobedience to God's fundamental principles about wealth, brings on desperation, and that makes people vulnerable to the temptations to take the Bribe. Christ's opponents are looking for such weakened people.

No matter what the currency, there is one big fact all the enemies of Christ agree about—the living Christ is the sole threat to their survival and success, and He must be stopped at all costs!

Chapter 4

Hush money

The cruel coalition of the Roman authorities and the religious elite could have killed the soldiers who knew the truth about Jesus' resurrection. Why didn't they? The likelihood is that the guards had something on the authorities.

The bribe was paid to get them to say Jesus' disciples stole His body, but anyway you cut it, the bribe was hush money. The establishment wanted the soldiers to keep quiet about the Resurrection, and secrets they might have known about the power-brokers who ran the government and religious system.

Then the lie, like all untruths, gained its own momentum across time.

Then the lie, like all untruths, gained its own momentum, and has snowballed across time. Matthew 28: 15 says, "So they took the money, and did as they were taught: and this saying is commonly reported among the Jews until this day" (KJV). Matthew's Gospel was written about 50 A.D., thus, as early as two decades after Christ's Resurrection, the lie was "commonly reported."

WIDESPREAD TODAY

Imagine how widespread it is today!

The bribe bought off people whose deity is "the god of this world" (2 Corinthians 4:4). Consider Mel Gibson, whose film, *The Passion of the Christ,* has earned more than $500 million, is ostracized and ignored by many in the cultural establishment. But the elites wrung their hands because they were not able to buy off the public that flocked to theaters to see the movie.

One Hollywood director who's a Christian said, "I don't make a big deal to my fellow workers about being a Christian, but it's amazing how people who are experiencing a divorce, or are having family or drug problems, always seem to seek me out." [1]

The hush money isn't working.

The official establishment in formerly communist lands found that out. When I first visited Ukraine and Russia in 1989, many still embraced the lie that had been promoted by communist authorities for 75 years. For three-quarters of a century, the people of those nations had been told by their elites that there is no God. But suddenly the light went on. With the collapse of communism, the truth rushed in. Many people discovered they had believed a lie. They found that not only does God exist, but He came in the Person of Jesus Christ.

People in the old communist world rushed into the Kingdom of God by the millions. And that goes for China, too, even though it hasn't given up totally on communism. David Aikman, former Beijing bureau chief for Time magazine, reported that a Chinese official was asked what he would decree for his nation if he had the authority to do so. The political leader shocked everybody with his answer: "It would be that China adopt Christianity as its main religion." [2]

The reason for the answer, says Aikman, is that "of all the world views, Christianity is most tolerant of scientific investigation and trade," both of which are very important to China right now. [3]

Throughout the world, individuals aren't buying the media's cheap tricks anymore. That's why there are so many "specials" and "documentaries" trying desperately to debunk the idea of Christ's Resurrection.

We've had *The Gospel of Judas* and *The Da Vinci Code* — along with the rehashing of a long-disproved "tomb" of Jesus and His family, and scores of other contrived attempts to discount the truth about Jesus.

More Coming

And we are likely to see more, since the promoters of the lie have to raise the ante to an increasingly intelligent and discerning audience that is beginning to see through their tactics.

> The immense cost of the bribe has been overwhelmed by the enormous price of salvation.

The reality is that when you have met the risen Jesus, like Paul on the side of the road, you're going to rejoice and be transformed by His living presence. With Job, you will shout, "I know that my Redeemer liveth..." Like the blind man, you will declare, "all I know is that once I was blind, but now I can see!"

The immense cost of the bribe has been overwhelmed by the enormous price of salvation—the precious blood of the Lamb of God. When you know that, no amount of hush money can shut you up.

I had never thought about the shocking amount that has

been spent through the centuries maintaining the bribe. Then, one day, while flying home from the African country of Ghana, I sensed the Lord speaking to me. "There's a bribe going on," I heard.

Initially, I thought this was a reference about a material bribe being paid. "Stop thinking in the natural," I felt the Lord was saying. "I'm telling you there's a bribe. Just look in My Word. Satan has had to bribe generation after generation." The price of the bribe has been raised higher and higher because people are getting more savvy—like those in China—and are beginning to recognize that the claims behind the bribe aren't true.

Scholars and scientists are awakening to the possibility that there is a Creator. Anthony Flew, Britain's most famous atheist, shocked many not long ago by claiming that the evidence no longer supports atheism. Way back in 1950, Flew, who became a non-believer at age 15, started writing about his atheistic beliefs. But, in his eighties, after all those decades of promoting unbelief, Flew said it had become too difficult in natural evolution to think about how the first reproducing organism came about.

Flew said he was committed to the principle of letting the evidence go where it leads, and that the evidence science has uncovered no longer supports atheism. [4]

While he said he wasn't becoming a biblical Christian, he now believes in the existence of God. Flew is not alone. One of the major debates in science is over "intelligent design," the reality that the universe had to have had a Creator. Some scientists are also accepting the idea of the "anthropic principle," the concept that the universe was designed specifically for human life.

Yet in Hollywood, Washington and the intellectual centers of the nation, many have worked hard to keep the bribe going for many years. In fact, one of the reasons liberals embrace the concept of tax-exempt status for churches is that it keeps them out of the political arena. To maintain their "non-profit" perks, churches have to silence their prophetic voices when it comes to specific politicians and their positions.

To maintain non-profit perks, churches have to silence their prophetic voices when it comes to specific politicians and their positions.

THE HARD WAY

The *Landmark Church* in Binghamton, New York, found this out the hard way. On October 30, 1992, the church took out full-page ads in USA Today and The Washington Times regarding the Bill Clinton campaign. "Christians Beware!" read the headline. Then the ads gave Clinton's position on issues important to evangelical Christians, like homosexuality and abortion. After a court battle, the church lost its tax exempt status. [5]

The elites in the establishment know that if the genuine church comes off the edges of the playing field, and into the arena itself, it will bring that prophetic truth against practices like abortion and sexual perversion.

Pastor Jeff Vanderstelt, of Tacoma, Washington, found a creative approach to the tax-exempt issue. World magazine tells the story:

> Pastor Jeff Vanderstelt of Soma Church in Tacoma, Wash., believes he may have a solution—one that doesn't involve bitter public lawsuits or backroom negotiations. For the past two years, Vanderstelt has paid every dime of property tax on his church's building as if it were a business. That's because it is.
>
> When the opportunity arose in 2005 for Soma to purchase the building in which it meets, Vanderstelt avoided typical church fundraising efforts. He took no special facilities offering and refused to sock his congregation with a massive mortgage. Instead, he established a for-profit LLC independent of the church and acquired financing from friendly investors at 8 percent interest.
>
> Consequently, Soma does not own its urban campus but leases it from Vanderstelt's company

at a highly discounted rate. And the church is not the only tenant. Telecommunications juggernaut AT&T and a private recording studio lease space in the building's basement, and other businesses periodically rent the facility for various events, generating enough income to completely cover the mortgage and tax burden. Last year, Vanderstelt's company operated in the black, donating its extra earnings to the church to provide salary raises for the staff. [6]

The cultural controllers earnestly don't want the Church out there in the public arena with them, so they do everything possible to keep the bribe rolling, including offering "carrots" to the Church, like tax exemption!

Chapter 5

E^{the}gyption
connection

The establishment elites today are willing to pay almost any price to keep people from knowing that Jesus rose from the dead and is alive. Those elites are no different from the ancient Roman civil authorities in Jerusalem or the religious leadership there in their passion to keep the Resurrection a secret.

When they fail to keep a lid on the truth, the cultural controllers try to stir doubt. They go all the way back to Genesis, and repeat the words of the serpent to Eve: "Hath God said?" In other words, the elites try to undermine the scriptural authority of the accounts of Jesus' Resurrection.

Though the bribe was paid first 2,000 years ago, its roots go back much farther. We can trace them through a strange biblical passage, which says, speaking of the two end-time witnesses,

When they have finished their testimony, the beast that comes up out of the abyss will make war with them, and overcome them and kill them. And their dead bodies will lie in the street of the great city which mystically is called Sodom and Egypt, where also their Lord was crucified (Revelation 11:7-8 NASU, emphasis added).

Mystically, Egypt is symbolic of a demonic stronghold, especially a spirit of unbelief. While Jerusalem was the literal place of Jesus' crucifixion—spiritually, it was the equivalent of Egypt, because of its unwillingness to believe in Jesus' Messiahship, and especially His Resurrection.

This unbelief, after all, was why the bribe was paid.

No wonder that, of the 600-plus references to Egypt in the Bible, 450 include the admonition to "come out" of Egypt. But rather than "coming out," modern American culture seems intent on going in deeper!

America seems infatuated with ancient Egypt. As the website Wikipedia says, "Since the early nineteenth century, the fascination with ancient Egypt seems to have affected every field of American culture." [1]

Just look at these examples:

- The Egyptian mummy became a symbol for people's fascination with reincarnation and life after death

- Las Vegas has been called America's "theme park." It seems to capture the nation's fascination. Old buildings have been torn down, and much in "sin city" is designed with an Egyptian flare.

- Go to the Rock and Roll Hall of Fame in Cleveland, and you will discover it's housed in a pyramid-shaped building.

- Travel down to Galveston, Texas, and you will see three pyramids housing a tourist attraction.

- The Washington Monument, towering over the Mall that stretches from the Lincoln Memorial to the Capitol, is an elongated pyramid.

- Even our currency carries the image of a pyramid.

- Also in Washington, the cornerstones of many buildings bear Egyptian symbols. The design was prompted by Masons, who influenced construction of the city. The Masons are among the most diabolically deceived groups on earth today, and then as now loved to mix a little bit of biblical religion with Egyptian folklore.

THE *Bribe* of Great Price •

- An amusement park in California is called "Pharaoh's Lost Kingdom." And of course there's Memphis, Tennessee, name for one of ancient Egypt's most notable cities.

Why this preoccupation with Egypt? Maybe it's an unconscious part of the bribe, to remind people and encourage them to continue to embrace the unbelief of which ancient Egypt is a symbol.

But the Bible brings much needed clarity about the "Egypt connection." The guards who knew the truth about Jesus' Resurrection were bribed to perpetuate unbelief, through the lie that the Lord's body had been snatched and hidden by His followers.

MAINTAINING CONFUSION

From that day until now, people still "pay" to keep this report confused, in doubt, and secretive. And the lie has been so cleverly crafted, and around so long, many don't recognize it as an untruth. This is why people have abandoned strong faith in the risen Christ, and turned to other religions. In fact, one major news magazine said that rather than being "one nation, under God," America is "one nation, under gods."

Richard Ostling, writing in Time, said, "The world has never seen a nation as religiously diverse as the U.S." Ostling went on to note that

> In addition to the various mainstream Judeo-Christian faiths that populated the original colonies, America now encompasses 700 to 800 "non-conventional" denominations, according to J. Gordon Melton, who monitors the proliferation for his Encyclopedia of American Religions. Half of them are imported variants of standard world religions, mostly Asian; the other half a creative and chaotic mix of U.S.-born creeds -- everything from Branch Davidians to New Agers. [2]

Rather **than** being "One **nation** under God," America **has** become **"One** nation under **gods."**

India's Hindus worship some three million "deities," but America may not be far behind. This is because many people have mixed religions and philosophies, and have found the brew so palatable they have lost taste for the truth. They have bought into the lie so completely they can't see through the disguise of unbelief.

They have been snared by the "Egypt Connection"!

Chapter 6

E^{the}gyptspirit

The truth is out and the idols are trembling.

Despite the attempts by cultural establishments across the ages, the bribe isn't working. People are awakening to the truth that Jesus is alive. This is why Buddhists, Hindus, and even Muslims are turning to Christ—often at immense risk. In fact, there are scores of people in underground churches in Iran, just as there have been in China for decades.

Charisma News Service reported the following in 2004:

Despite tragedy and persecution, a vibrant underground church is growing in Iran, according to Charisma Now (June 29, 2004). After an earthquake on December 26 devastated Bam and buried thousands of people under the rubble of their homes, Western churches sent relief to the ancient Iranian city. Today, the church in Iran is growing. Missions experts estimate 20,000-30,000 indigenous evangelical and Pentecostal believers today, most of them from Muslim backgrounds. Some experts - citing an unknown number of "secret" believers - claim the true figure could be much higher. "In the last 20 years, more Iranians have come to Christ compared to the last 14 centuries," Lazarus Yeghnazar, 55, an Iranian-born evangelist now based in Great Britain, told "Charisma" magazine in its June issue. "We've never seen such a phenomenal thirst," he added. Missiologist Patrick Johnstone, co-author of "Operation World," estimated that Iran has 17,000 evangelicals, 7,000 Charismatics and 4,000 Pentecostals. With annual church growth of 7.5 percent, Pentecostalism is the fastest-growing religious movement in Iran. Everywhere, the charismatic influence is strong. Many indigenous churches practice prophecy and healing. Services, which are marked by vibrant worship and fervent prayer, can last for hours.

The people of such churches know the truth, and the old idols they've followed are shaking, just as Isaiah said they would, when he wrote, under the inspiration of the Holy Spirit, these prophetic words,

> "Behold, the LORD is riding on a swift cloud and is about to come to Egypt; The idols of Egypt will tremble at His presence, And the heart of the Egyptians will melt within them."
>
> —ISAIAH 19:1 NASU

AN IDOL IS 'NOTHING'

Paul tells us that an idol is "nothing," an empty structure. However, demons find a place of habitation in the idol. Jesus always made the demons quake, and that's why the truth of His Resurrection makes the idols shake where the demons lodge.

And the more the truth spreads and the idols tremble, the more the world raises the ante to sustain the bribe.

The lie has been passed down from generation to generation, played and replayed a thousand times in a thousand different ways. And again and again, God calls His covenant people out of "Egypt."

Paul describes this mentality accurately when he writes about "every lofty thing raised up against the knowledge of God" (2 Corinthians 10:5). This is the spirit of "Egyptian" idolatry. It's a system of unbelief, paid for by the bribe, and perpetuating more bribes.

The system spins replacement religions, like sex, drug addictions, materialism, and a host of other substitutes for true worship. "Do not get drunk with wine, for that is dissipation, but be filled with the Spirit," Paul writes in Ephesians 5:18 (NAS). Nevertheless, multitudes prefer the intoxicants to the Spirit.

These false belief systems that the bribe pays for provide people a measure of truth—just enough to make them appear reputable—but steer away from absolutes. In their confused thinking, absolutes can't exist.

Especially the absolute truth about Jesus and His Resurrection.

If they concede an inch, the facts will have to be recorded in history books, in science publications, and public schools will have to teach factually that a Man rose from the dead. Abortion and euthanasia will have to stop, as will all other criminal and immoral behaviors sanctioned by the elites. At all costs, the establishment elites have to keep paying the bribe so the absolute truth about Jesus Christ will remain concealed from the masses.

The lie must be exalted above the truth, in the style of Lucifer, who said,

> "I will ascend to heaven; I will raise my throne above the stars of God, And I will sit on the mount of assembly In the recesses of the north. I will ascend above the heights of the clouds; I will make myself like the Most High."
>
> —ISAIAH 14:13-14 NASU

This is the scam the devil has always pushed on the world—being "like the Most High." That luciferian spirit is what drives the "Egypt" mentality. It is the passion for fame and fortune to human beings that they, too, can be exalted if they will accept the bribe and believe the lie.

But through the Holy Spirit, the Prophet Ezekiel saw through the sham. God tells him,

> "Son of man, say to Pharaoh king of Egypt and to his hordes, 'Whom are you like in your greatness?'" ... "I made the

This is **the scam** the devil **has** always **pushed** on the **world, being** like the Most **High** God.

nations quake at the sound of its fall when
I made it go down to Sheol with those who
go down to the pit; and all the well-watered
trees of Eden, the choicest and best of
Lebanon, were comforted in the earth beneath. They also went down with it to Sheol
to those who were slain by the sword; and
those who were its strength lived under its
shade among the nations. To which among
the trees of Eden are you thus equal in glory and greatness? Yet you will be brought
down with the trees of Eden to the earth beneath; you will lie in the midst of the uncir-
cumcised, with those who were slain by the
sword. So is Pharaoh and all his hordes!"'
declares the Lord GOD."

—EZEKIEL 31:2, 16-18 NASU

The prophet here likens Lucifer to Egypt's pharaoh. The
point is that the spirit of Egypt is an earthly manifestation of
the sin and fall of Lucifer and his hosts.

The arrogance of this spirit, which underlies the bribe, is
seen again in Ezekiel:

"Son of man, set your face against Pharaoh
king of Egypt and prophesy against him and
against all Egypt. Speak and say, 'Thus says
the Lord GOD, "Behold, I am against you,

> Pharaoh king of Egypt, The great monster
> that lies in the midst of his rivers, That has
> said, 'My Nile is mine, and I myself have
> made it."
>
> —EZEKIEL 29:2-3

The Nile was the most powerful river in the known world in Ezekiel's day. No Nile, no Egypt. The picture he presents is that of a huge serpentine monster lying in the river, believing it not only to be its home, but its creation. This is the zenith of arrogance, and a crowning example of the lying spirit behind the bribe.

Expanded, the deceiving monster is claiming that he is the source of the vitality of society, the supplier of prosperity. This is the delusion the lying beast fosters in places like Wall Street and Las Vegas. People, like Ezekiel's river-monster, believe human beings alone created the world they enjoy.

EMBRACE 'REASON' NOT REVELATION

In 1933, 34 humanists came together to write a statement of their beliefs. The document was called The Humanist Manifesto. The statement wanted to lay down a challenge to Christians especially, to lay down their beliefs based on revelation and embrace reason as the source of all truth.

Forty years later, in 1973, a group of humanists issued a new Manifesto. There, they stated,

> As in 1933, humanists still believe that traditional theism, especially faith in the prayer-hearing God, assumed to live and care for persons, to hear and understand their prayers, and to be able to do something about them, is an unproved and outmoded faith. Salvationism, based on mere affirmation, still appears as harmful, diverting people with false hopes of heaven hereafter. Reasonable minds look to other means for survival... we can discover no divine purpose or providence for the human species. While there is much that we do not know, humans are responsible for what we are or will become. No deity will save us; we must save ourselves. [1]

The conclusion, as Humanist Manifesto II put it in 1973, is that people don't need God, and that man can be his own savior. So the assumption is that the nation doesn't need God in its educational systems or in its political and governing institutions.

Like the Nile-monster, people shout, "We can create and build anything because we are so powerful." So Egypt's pharaoh's doubtless looked at their giant pyramids, and succumbed to the delusion. The prophet speaks not only against the ruler, but "all Egypt." Those who embrace the lying system fall under the condemnation and judgment of holy God, just as their satanic leader does.

In God's eyes, the spirit of Egypt is the spirit of a city and of a man who says he can do everything himself.

This attitude extends to the religious establishment. Today there are more churches in America than any time in history. There are more Christian TV programs, more Christian books, and more Christian ministries than ever. More people attend churches on Sunday mornings in big cities like Dallas, Houston and Atlanta, yet those cities are continually in moral decline, crime is up and divorce rates are rising. In the area of my city, Baltimore, there are some 1,400 churches, yet our murder rate stays in the top 10 of all America's cities.

We're **trying** to **dress** up **the** Church with **new** **ideas** and approaches to **make** it more **attractive.**

If the Church is the answer to the culture and society—the salt and light principle—then why isn't change happening?

We're often addressing our method when it's our message that's wrong. We're trying to dress up the Church with new ideas and approaches to make it more attractive. Well, you can dress up a pig but it's still a pig. We must change our message and entire approach to living the life of the Kingdom of God if we're going to see real change take place.

We have preached the separation of the church from the world so much (with the secular world's problems consistently our message) that we no longer fit into the world we're trying to impact. We have our Christian TV, radio and music awards. Soon, I suppose, we'll have our own Christian Miss America Pageant.

> We must **preach** the Gospel of the **Kingdom** and not just the Gospel of Salvation.

Enough! I don't believe this was Jesus' plan when He walked this earth.

We need to put ourselves in every facet of society—education, politics, the arts, entertainment, finance, and all the rest. We must stop preaching separation from sin as separation from society. We can live out our born-again, Christian lives without compromise in every part of society.

We must preach the Gospel of the Kingdom and not just the Gospel of Salvation. We must change our message from separation from the world and culture to infiltrating and influencing our world and culture.

We need to invade that world with His life and love, through a real demonstration of His anointing in our lives so that we can become the best at whatever we put our hands to do, all that He might be glorified.

That will truly break "Egypt's" bondage off the Church!

Chapter 7

Under
the spell

Modern America is woozy with the spell of Egypt. Our nation is drunk with pride, arrogance and unbelief.

It's vital we heed the warnings God gives through Ezekiel:

> "I will turn the fortunes of Egypt and make them return to the land of Pathros, to the land of their origin, and there they will be a lowly kingdom. It will be the lowest of the kingdoms, and it will never again lift itself up above the nations. And I will make

Our nation is drunk with pride, arrogance, and unbelief.

them so small that they will not rule over the nations ... The word of the LORD came again to me saying, "Son of man, prophesy and say, Thus says the Lord GOD, "Wail, 'Alas for the day!' For the day is near, Even the day of the LORD is near; It will be a day of clouds, A time of doom for the nations.

A sword will come upon Egypt, And anguish will be in Ethiopia; When the slain fall in Egypt, They take away her wealth, And her foundations are torn down. Ethiopia, Put, Lud, all Arabia, Libya and the people of the land that is in league will fall with them by the sword." 'Thus says the LORD, "Indeed, those who support Egypt will fall And the pride of her power will come down; From Migdol to Syene They will fall within her by the sword," Declares the Lord GOD. They will be desolate In the midst of the desolated lands; And her cities will be In the midst of the devastated cities. And they will know that I am the LORD, When I set a fire in Egypt And all her helpers are broken."

—EZEKIEL 29:14-15; 30:1-8

Under
the spell

One example shows how dangerous it is for our nation—any nation—to be under the spell of ancient Egypt, with its pride, arrogance and bribe-paid unbelief. David Barton has done extensive research about what happened after the Supreme Court ruled school prayer unconstitutional in 1962. Barton traces the rise of sexual disorder and the decline of academics as prayer was removed, as follows: [1]

Since 1963:

- Premarital sexual activity increased over 200 percent (for girls alone, premarital sexual activity increased over 500 percent);

- Pregnancies to unwed mothers went up almost 400 percent;

- Gonorrhea (Sexually Transmitted Disease) went up over 200 percent;

- Number of suicides increased over 400 percent.

These give rise to secondary consequences, such as:

- Only half of those who give birth before age 18 complete high school (as compared with 96 percent of those who postpone childbearing);

- On average they earn half as much money and are far more likely to be dependent on welfare. A negative cycle is created, with daughters falling pregnant during teenage years, thus leading to generations of unskilled peoples being dependent and trapped on welfare;

- Of those families headed by a mother age 14-25, two-thirds live below the poverty level.

- Teenage pregnancies cost the public 16.65 billion in 1985 alone.

The banning of prayer in school assemblies, affected academic achievement.

The banning of prayer in school assemblies affected academic achievement:

The Scholastic Aptitude Test (SAT) is an academic test measuring the developed verbal and mathematical reasoning skills of a student preparing to enter college. The three areas of SAT testing with individual documentation are SAT mathematics scores, SAT verbal scores, and SAT total scores (the combination of the mathematics and verbal scores).

SAT Total Scores have declined steadily, dropping over 90 points from 1963 to 1980 (the lowest in the industrialized world). Although actual grades have risen, their SATS were decreasing. Hence academic standards have dropped to accommodate mediocrity.

In 1950, 84 percent of college students knew that Manila

was the capital of the Philippines. In 1984 it had dropped to only 27 percent. We cannot expect to be a world leader if our populace doesn't even know who the rest of the world is.

SAT scores began to improve in 1981 (after 17 years of continual decline). However this increase was attributed to the increase in private Christian schooling and home-schooling. Although in 1986, private schooling only made up 12,4% of the school going population, their academic performance was 3 to 5 times greater than their size (i.e. the number of top academic achievers came disproportionately from these private Christian schools). Some have argued that their greater academic performance is due to greater family affluence. However, studies confirm that parents who send their children to private schools have an income only marginally greater than the national average. Furthermore, in 1986 the average private school spent $1,100 per student annually as compared to the average public school's annual expenditure of $3,752 per student. Yet private Christian schools produce three times more academic achievers at a third of the price. A very plausible answer is that prayer is not banned in private Christian schools.

The banning of prayer in school assemblies affected moral standards:

The **banning** of prayer in **school** assemblies, **affected** moral **standards.**

Before prayer was removed from schools, polls among educators listed the top offences in public schools as:

- Talking; Chewing gum; Making noise; Running in the halls; Getting out of turn in line; Wearing improper clothing; Not putting paper in wastebaskets.

After prayer was removed from schools, polls among educators listed the top offences in public schools as:

- Rape; Robbery; Assault; Burglary; Arson; Bombings; Murder; Suicide; Absenteeism; Vandalism; Extortion; Drug abuse; Alcohol abuse; Gang warfare; Pregnancies; Abortions; Venereal disease;

None of the previous top seven problems even make the list.

The banning of prayer in assemblies affected families:

The banning of prayer in school assemblies, affected families.

Stability existed in the family during the years that students prayed daily for their families, however, since praying for families was banned:

- Divorce went up almost 120 percent;

- Single parent families went up 140 percent;

- Unmarried couples living together increased over 350 percent;

• Adultery increased nearly 300 percent.

These give rise to secondary consequences, such as:

• A dramatic increase in youth running away from home. All research points to basic family instability, such as divorce, single parent families, unmarried couples living together and adultery, as being the primary cause.

• Family breakdown is also associated with increase in physical and sexual abuse.

The banning of prayer in assemblies affected school violence:

In 1985, on average, 24 teachers and 215 students were assaulted every day in California schools.

Furthermore a 1978 study revealed:

The **banning** of **prayer** in **school** assemblies, **affected** violence.

• Risk of violence to teenagers is greater in public schools than anywhere else.

• Nearly 2.5 million of the nation's secondary school students had something worth more than a dollar stolen from them in a month.

• An estimated 282,000 secondary school students

reported they were attacked at school in a typical one-month period.

The high levels of violence in public schools equally affect teachers:

- 5,200 were physically attacked in the period of one month.
- Nearly one-fifth of the attacks required medical treatment.
- Attacks on teachers were almost five times as likely to result in serious injury as attacks on students.

The banning of prayer in assemblies affected the state of the nation:

The banning of prayer in school assemblies, affected the state of the Nation.

Since 1962:

- The rate of violent crime has risen over 500 percent;
- National productivity has dropped over 80 percent;
- The per capita alcohol consumption has increased by 35 percent.

In fact, when you look at the specific prayer that riled the Court, it's downright chilling. It was composed by the New York Board of Regents, and said the following: "Almighty God, we acknowledge our dependence upon thee, and we beg Thy blessings upon us, our parents, our teachers and our Country."

The outlawing of such a request to God revealed just how intoxicated America's highest court and judicial system was with its arrogance and pride. They didn't take away bricks or textbooks or marking boards. The educators added computers, but removed prayer. All the elements they kept couldn't stop the slide into the chaos of modern public education in America.

And the bribe keeps rolling in, trying to keep people quiet about the removal of communion with God from the public educational system.

Egypt represents a spirit of selective unbelief—you can believe in "gods," but not the true and living God. Actors and other public figures are well-received talking about their faith in Buddha or New Age cults, but believers in the genuine God are marginalized and ostracized.

But many discover they can have it both ways—a little bit of Jehovah God and a pinch of this religion and that. This is what's behind so many popular belief systems today, and it's sheer deception.

More than that, it's dangerous. When you don't know which deity you are praying to, you can get an answer from anybody. Demons can manifest themselves as "angels of light"

(2 Corinthians 11:14). Worshipping at these idolatrous thrones, people actually wind up giving their hearts to demons, and come under demonic control and influence.

JUDE SOUNDS THE ALARM

No wonder Jude sounds an alarm to all who are teased with the spirit of Egypt: Now I desire to remind you, though you know all things once for all, that the Lord, after saving a people out of the land of Egypt, subsequently destroyed those who did not believe (Jude 5).

Many of the Hebrews who had been liberated from Egypt hankered to go back. They forgot they had built magnificent Egyptian cities and monuments under the whip. Out in the wilderness, though, they seemed to have fallen into a fantasy that they would go back to Egypt and sit on the banks of the Nile sipping lemonade.

But the seducing influence of the Egypt-spirit is so great many of the Hebrews want to go back, despite the 400 years of torment and misery they had experienced in Egypt. The contradiction is striking: their shackles had been loosed, but they wanted to abandon the living God and go back to the land of their enslavement!

The spirit of Egypt is powerful. That's why so many people across the centuries have been willing to accept the bribe of unbelief.

Now we understand better the text referred to earlier, that Jesus was crucified in "Sodom and Egypt." It's because Jerusalem, the religious capital of Israel, was so perverted with the spirit of Egypt and Sodom that it was the equivalent of those places in God's eyes. The religious veneer was a thin cover over the underlying system of power politics, religious positions and titles, and the refusal to believe and truly trust God. In addition, there had been a normalization of practices condemned in Sodom and Gomorrah.

As I write, one of the controversies from the "Holy Land" making the news is the use of near-naked models to lure tourists to Israel. Sincere believers were appalled, but the secular press howled.

Even today, when I have visited Israel, I have felt the spirit of perversion. I don't like religion and religion doesn't like me, yet the religious spirit is everywhere.

Two thousand years ago, the soldiers at the tomb were bribed by the religious leaders.

Why would ancient Israel want to go back to Egypt, why would modern Israel want to be wrapped up in the religious spirit, and why do so many people buy into the bribe that addicts them to the spirit of Egypt?

It's because one lie begets another lie. Two thousand years ago, the soldiers at the tomb were bribed by the religious leaders. They were told that if the governor found out the truth, they would simply cover it over with more lies.

And all this would be done through the passing of money. Shekels, gold and dollar bills add value and money attaches the thing lied about to the earth. As it is worked into the earth, the bribe-bought lie becomes almost second nature to earth's inhabitants.

When a person is under the spell of Egypt, it's almost impossible to see the truth.

Chapter 8

Swimming
in the cesspool

Swim in a cesspool long enough, and you may become desensitized to its stench.

This is why so many people accept the bribe and no longer see the lie it promotes. Many have been swimming in a cesspool of deceit and delusion for so long they no longer are aware of the pungent odor of its deceits.

A feature of our culture is that we enshrine lies in academic nobility until we believe them as truth. Nothing illustrates this as graphically as Darwinism. Though a number studies and books, authored by experts, have recently shown the flaws in evolution, it is still promoted as absolute truth.

Michael Behe, in fact, stirred the scientific world with the publication of his book, Darwin's Black Box. Dr. Ray Bohlin summarized Behe's thesis this way:

Behe's simple claim is that when Darwin wrote The Origin of Species, the cell was a mysterious black box. We could see the outside of it, but we had no idea of how it worked. In Origin, Darwin stated,

> If it could be demonstrated that any complex organ existed, which could not possibly have been formed by numerous, successive, slight modifications, my theory would absolutely break down. But I can find no such case.

> Simply put, Behe has found such a case. Behe claims that with the opening of the black box of the cell through the last 40 years of research in molecular and cell biology, there are now numerous examples of complex molecular machines that absolutely break down the theory of natural selection as an all-encompassing explanation of living systems. The power and logic of his examples prompted Christianity Today to name Darwin's Black

Box as their 1996 Book of the Year. Quite a
distinction for a book on science published by
a secular publisher! [1]

If someone in the scientific field departs from their "true
religion" of Darwinism, they are marginalized and cast aside.
An editor of a major American scientific journal found that out
the hard way when he was fired for being a creationist.

BODY OF LIES

It's easy to create a body of lies and make it appear as a towering citadel of truth if one pays out the bribe long enough, and to enough people. So the bribe of acceptance, awards and position are paid to the educational and scientific establishments to propagate the notion of our descent from monkeys.

It's easy to create a body of lies and make it appear as a towering citadel of truth.

No one should be surprised at the "findings" television
documentaries will breathlessly announce linking us to the
apes. Archaeology will make "discoveries" that can be contrived
to confirm Darwinism, and media will present it as fact.

Millions will accept the bribe, and the lie will grow and
deepen its poisonous roots in the lore of learning.

However, let a discovery be made that confirms the authenticity of Scripture, and it will be covered up like a coffin under six feet of hard earth. If Noah's Ark is found on the slopes of Ararat, the news must be hushed. If science discovers that the Shroud of Turin really was Jesus' burial cloth, and the figure was emblazoned in its fabric by the energy of His Resurrection, the discovery must be silenced—or banished to religious TV channels only. If the Ark of the Covenant is found, the news must never get out.

In short, anything that threatens the lie and promises to rescue people from its cesspool must be kept from public view. A whiff of fresh air might make too many realize they are swimming in muck.

One of the favorite forms of spreading the lie is by re-defining the language.

One of the favorite forms of spreading the lie is by re-defining language. "Abortion" is not the killing of an infant by burning it alive with a chemical or slicing its living body with a surgical instrument, or piercing its brain with scissors. Instead, it is cloaked in a more acceptable compromise— the word "choice." Perverted sexuality is not named as such, but is called the "gay" lifestyle.

So many people have been swimming for so long in all

those cesspools that it smells pretty good to them. Anyone who suggests otherwise is considered an extremist and deemed crazy. Some are packed off to a counselor, or, in the case of "hate crimes," to jail.

So what are we in the Church to do? It's clear: We must recover our prophetic voice. We must stand up and yell out loud. If we saw people swimming in a sewer, surely we would warn them that they're in danger of disease. That's the condition of our culture, and that's why we must sound the alarm of truth.

REASSERT TESTIMONY POWER

This is critically true regarding the Resurrection of our Lord. To overwhelm the bribe and crush the lie, we must assert the power of our testimony. The greatest proof of the Resurrection of Jesus Christ was the transformed lives of the early disciples. Men who wouldn't go to the foot of Jesus' cross for fear of the military and religious establishments were now willing to die on crosses themselves because they had met the living Christ.

> The transforming work of Jesus hasn't stopped, because He's alive.

And the transforming work of Jesus Christ hasn't stopped, because He's alive. Our role is to testify prophetically to the Resurrection with the declarations, "I met

Him! He touched me. He changed me! He's alive!"

Once that story gets out—and it is—there's no way to get it back in the bottle. Let people everywhere—at home, work, school, in social groups, at church—know that Jesus Christ is alive in your life.

As they see that they will suddenly recognize they've been swimming in a cesspool. The lie and its bribe will become repugnant to them, and they will scamper out like a person discovering he's swimming with piranhas.

Religion leaves people in the cesspool because all it offers is dry theology and empty ritual. There's no fragrance there except the smell of death.

But when the fragrance of the risen Christ hits somebody's nostrils, they immediately distinguish it from the odor of the cesspool. Paul puts it like this,

> For we are a fragrance of Christ to God among those who are being saved and among those who are perishing; to the one an aroma from death to death, to the other an aroma from life to life...
>
> —2 CORINTHIANS 2:15-16

Notice the passage doesn't say, "Theology is a fragrance of Christ," or "liturgy is a fragrance of Christ." Rather, it says we are that lovely smell. The delightful aroma is that of our testimony, our declaration of a changing life, brought about by the risen Lord.

There are those who have been in the cesspool of lies so long they find the testimony of Christ repugnant. Maybe these are the folk who have committed the unpardonable sin. The testimony of the truth about Christ's Resurrection is death to them, because they will not repent, and it only confirms their eternal destiny of Hell.

But to those who will receive the truth, there's deliverance from the cesspool. And no amount of money, or any other form of bribe, can compare to the glorious brightness and purity of light found in the fact that Jesus is alive indeed!

the BIG deal about unbelief

So what's the big deal about unbelief anyway? Why is there such a determination to keep the bribe going so people won't accept, believe in and rest their lives on Jesus Christ and His Resurrection?

When you check out key Bible verses detailing the results of unbelief, it's easy to see why the satanic system is so determined to keep paying the bribe so people won't believe.

'SPURNING' OF GOD

First, unbelief is a "spurning" of God. We see this is Numbers 14:11, which tells us, "The LORD said to Moses, 'How long will this people spurn Me? And how long will they not believe in Me, despite all the signs which I have performed in their midst?'"

"Spurn" means to "despise" and "abhor." When you think about the heart of God, you can see how badly unbelief grieves Him. All through the Bible, God is revealed as a lover in pursuit of His beloved. The Bible presents Israel as the "apple" of His eye. It reveals that Hosea's rebellious wife Gomer is a type of Israel's rejection of God. In the New Testament, the Church is described as His bride.

The devil delights in bringing grief to the heart of God.

Can anything be as hurtful to a man desperately in love with the woman of his dreams, than for her to despise and abhor him? Yet this is what unbelief is to the heart of God!

The devil delights in bringing grief to God's heart, and is willing to pay out any amount to keep bribing people—especially the Church—to stay in unbelief.

Unbelief brings on God's judgment. We discover this in many passages, including Psalm 78, which says,

the BIG deal
about unbelief

> "Therefore the LORD heard and was full of
> wrath; And a fire was kindled against Jacob
> And anger also mounted against Israel, Be-
> cause they did not believe in God And did
> not trust in His salvation"
> —PSALM 78:21-22 NASU

Wrath and love are closely linked. The reason is that love involves passion, and God's love is so immense that He is also immensely passionate. In addition, love will do all that's possible to avoid rejection, but ultimately true love permits the freedom of the beloved, including suffering the consequences of rebellion.

Not only does unbelief hurt God's heart, but it impacts the person who rejects God. Isaiah records God words, "If you will not believe, you surely shall not last" (Isaiah 7:9 NASU). Unbelief weakens our ability to endure, persevere and hold out against the assaults and challenges of the enemy.

Unbelief quenches the power of the Holy Spirit to bring us the blessings of our loving God. At Nazareth, Jesus "did not do many miracles... because of their unbelief" (Matthew 13:58). The "Nazareth syndrome" blocks many of the works of God that people need desperately.

In fact, in light of all He had said and done, which the people had heard and seen, Jesus "wondered at their unbelief" (Mark 6:6). Today, we can't help but wonder what else God has to do to convince people of His great love and mercy. In light of the transformation of individuals and whole societies under the power of the risen Christ, it's a wonder there are still people accepting the bribe, and continuing in their unbelief!

DISCIPLES INCLUDED

That number includes Jesus' closest disciples 2,000 years ago, as Mark reports:

> Afterward He appeared to the eleven them-
> selves as they were reclining at the table;
> and He reproached them for their unbelief
> and hardness of heart, because they had not
> believed those who had seen Him after He
> had risen.
>
> —MARK 16:14 NASU

Today, significant portions of the Church fall into unbelief. Some have spurned the authority of the Bible. They have set aside its doctrines—especially those that contemporary culture finds uncomfortable. Theological movements have fallen into apostasy, denying the Resurrection.

Way back in the 17th century, German theologians came up with the idea of submitting the Bible to the same techniques of textual criticism as any other work of literature. One of them even said he was reacting to the notion of the "supernatural"—which he didn't like.

The movement spread, impacting many churches and denominations. It began to blossom among liberals in America in the 1920s. Norman Vincent Peale, one of the preachers under the influences that undermined biblical authority told Phil Donahue that he didn't think it was necessary to be born again. Christ, he said, is merely "one of the ways" to God." [1]

Apostasy took a heavy toll on the American Episcopal Church. One of its bishops, John Spong, wrote books explaining why he didn't believe in foundational doctrines like the Virgin Birth and Resurrection of Christ.

What's really scary is that Israel was "broken off for their unbelief" (Romans 11:20). This doesn't mean God stopped loving Israel or having that special place in His "eye" for her. But it does mean that unbelief cut Israel off from the unique intimacy the bride has with the groom, and the protection and provision that accompany it.

If unbelief resulted in those consequences for the "apple" of God's eye, be assured that accepting the bribe and persisting in unbelief will cut us off from the rich and saving relationship

The promise land strands across time as the symbol of the richness of God's kingdom living.

with God and the bounty of Heaven.

This is because unbelief keeps us from entering into the Land of Promise (Hebrews 3:19). The "Promised Land" stands across time as the symbol of the richness of God's Kingdom living. But unbelief keeps us from going into the position of prosperity, peace, protection and providence, just as it kept the ancient Hebrews from entering into God's rest. They were in the land, but they were striving there, rather than relying on God. Instead, they expressed their unbelief by worshipping the "gods" of the land.

WHAT UNBELIEF IS

If unbelief is such a big deal to our enemy, we need to consider what unbelief is. That brings us back to our original questions: What's the big deal about unbelief and why is so much spent on the bribe to maintain the lie?

- Unbelief is a holdout to the satanic promise, "ye shall be as gods," since it puts a person's reason above revelation.

Remember, this was the serpent's key strategy for convincing Adam and Eve to rebel against God. All the devil had to do was introduce the deadly ambition to exalt himself above God, a goal that had gotten him cast out of Heaven.

Whatever has the ability to accurately judge something else

is superior to whatever it judges. If reason is the judge of true revelation, then you have to conclude that reason has more authority than revelation.

So, to apply reason to determine whether or not the Bible is true is a form of unbelief, since it begins with the assumption that it may not be true, and only human reason can tell the difference.

An example of this arrogance is found in the "Jesus Seminar," made up of liberal theologians who meet and vote on what they think Jesus "really" said and did (based on a basic disbelief regarding the reliability of the Bible). Dr. William Lane Craig, a critic of the Jesus Seminar, summed up their ideas like this:

> The real, historical Jesus turns out to have been a sort of itinerant, social critic, the Jewish equivalent of a Greek cynic philosopher. He never claimed to be the Son of God or to forgive sins or to inaugurate a new covenant between God and man. His crucifixion was an accident of history; his corpse was probably thrown into a shallow dirt grave where it rotted away or was eaten by wild dogs. [2]

People like those in the Jesus Seminar and apostate churches actually have a greater faith in human reason than they do belief in the Bible!

- Unbelief is an obstacle to having a life transformed by Jesus Christ.

The simple fact is that many people become agnostics or atheists because they don't want a transformed life. They think that kind of life will take away their "good times" through sex and partying.

Some of them go through high-sounding arguments to try to justify their unbelief. Freud, the founder of psychoanalysis, was an atheist who said God was merely a dream in the human brain. The human being was nothing more than a body in search of sex or trying to resolve sexually-related problems.

When a person believes in Jesus Christ, and commits his life to Christ, the Holy Spirit comes to live inside the person. The Spirit begins to transform the individual's thinking and behavior.

Unbelief keeps this from happening.

- If belief is "leaning on" and "casting weight" on God, then unbelief is putting all a person's confidence in man, which is an indirect way of leaning on the devil.

The Greek word that appears in the New Testament, translated "belief" or "faith," and sometimes "trust," means to set down all your weight on something. When you or I sit down in a chair, we "believe" it will hold us.

Since that's what "belief" means, then its opposite—unbelief—would mean an unwillingness to trust in something, in this case, God and His Word.

But the problem is that absolute unbelief is impossible. Everybody believes in something. The unbeliever is placing all his weight on the possibility there is no God, or that the Bible isn't true, or that Jesus didn't rise from the dead.

Absolute unbelief is impossible. Everybody believes in something.

It's foolhardy to trust a person's whole eternity to such flimsy faith in unbelief!

George Bernard Shaw found that out. He was one of the world's leading unbelievers, and did all he could to undermine the faith of others. But late in life, Shaw wrote,

> "The science to which I pinned my faith is bankrupt. Its counsels, which should have established the millennium, led instead, directly to the suicide of Europe. I believed them once. In their name I helped to destroy the faith of millions of worshippers in the temples of a thousand creeds. And now they look at me and witness the great tragedy of an atheist who has lost his faith." [3]

THE *Bribe* of Great Price •

Shaw was one of the agents doling out the bribe through his books, articles and speeches. In the end, however, he discovered he could no longer live with his unbelief.

Way back in 1936, Arthur Guiterman wrote a poem describing the slide into modern unbelief. He didn't intend to be prophetic, but the poem accurately described what would happen:

> First dentistry was painless;
> Then bicycles were chainless
> And carriages were horseless
> And many laws, enforce-less.
> Next, cookery was fireless,
> Telegraphy was wireless,
> Cigars were nicotine-less
> And coffee, caffeine-less.
> Soon oranges were seedless,
> The putting green was weed-less,
> The college boy hatless,
> The proper diet, fatless,
> Now motor roads are dustless,
> The latest steel is rust-less,
> Our tennis courts are sod-less,
> Our new religions, godless. [4]

Chapter 10

the BIG deal about the Resurrection

Unquestionably, as I have tried to show throughout this book, the whole point of paying the bribe is to keep people from believing in the Resurrection of Jesus Christ.

What's the big deal about the Resurrection?

- Faith in Jesus Christ stands or falls on the truth of the Resurrection.

Paul writes that "if Christ was not raised, then all our preaching is useless, and your trust in God is useless." (1 Corinthians 15:14 NLT)

Faith in Jesus Christ stands or falls on the truth of the resurrection.

The Resurrection isn't an "add-on," placed there by Jesus' followers years after His earthly ministry. It is the very core of biblical belief. And it's not just a belief that Christ "lives on" through His impact on people and events, but that Jesus literally and physically rose from the dead.

If the devil can bribe enough people into believing that Christ didn't rise again, then he will have destroyed the heart of faith and proven the Bible to be a myth. As you can see, the stakes are enormous for the prince of darkness and his demonic hosts!

- Personal transformation is hopeless apart from the Resurrection of Jesus Christ.

In Romans 5, Paul shows again just how important the Resurrection is:

> Much more then, having now been justified by His blood, we shall be saved from the wrath of God through Him. For if while we were enemies we were reconciled to God through the death of His Son, much more, having been reconciled, we shall be saved by His life."
>
> —ROMANS 5:9-10 NASU

Some might think it was enough for Jesus to die as our substitute, taking the penalty for our sins. But why did the Resurrection have to occur? It messes up things for the rational mind. After all, we can all imagine somebody dying. But rising from the dead? Not likely, says human reason.

However, there is no transformation of our lives, in this world, if Christ isn't risen. He transfers the power of His life to us. We are justified in the Father's eyes the moment we receive Christ as Savior. That's an event, described as a "birth."

But when we receive Christ as Lord, we are taking in His whole life. This launches the transforming process known as sanctification. Gradually, more and more of the territory of our lives is turned over to Him.

But if He's dead, there's no transforming life available for us!

- If Christ is not risen, we would have dead religion, not living hope.

Peter wrote,

> "Blessed be the God and Father of our Lord Jesus Christ, who according to His great mercy has caused us to be born again to a living hope through the resurrection of Jesus Christ from the dead..."
>
> —1 Peter 1:3 NASU

"Living" is from the Greek word, zoë. Two words in the original language of the New Testament are translated "life." Bios means fleshly, material and temporary existence. Zoë refers to life as God has it—perfect, eternal, indestructible.

If Christ is not risen, we have no power for living.

If Christ is not risen, all we have is bios—existence in time and space. And that means all we've got is dead religion, not a living hope. "Hope" refers to something you expect to happen, not a faint wish like winning a super lottery. If Christ is risen, then all the wonderful blessings of God are before us, and we anticipate receiving them!

• If Christ is not risen, we have no power for living.

Paul said in Philippians 3:10 that his great passion was to "know him, and the power of his resurrection, and the fellowship of his sufferings…" (emphasis added)

A religion that got you ready to die but offered no strength for living would be inadequate and incomplete. That's the kind of religion we would have if Jesus hadn't risen from the dead.

Look at the power for living the resurrection hope gave to Paul:

> For God, who said, "Light shall shine out of darkness," is the One who has shone in our

hearts to give the Light of the knowledge of
the glory of God in the face of Christ. But
we have this treasure in earthen vessels, so
that the surpassing greatness of the power
will be of God and not from ourselves; we
are afflicted in every way, but not crushed;
perplexed, but not despairing; persecuted,
but not forsaken; struck down, but not destroyed; always carrying about in the body
the dying of Jesus, so that the life of Jesus
also may be manifested in our body. For
we who live are constantly being delivered
over to death for Jesus' sake, so that the life
of Jesus also may be manifested in our mor-
tal flesh.

—2 CORINTHIANS 4:6-11 NASU

In fact, our power comes from being filled up, with the Holy
Spirit. In Ephesians 5:18, he says we're not to get drunk with wine,
but filled with the Spirit. An intoxicant influences and ignites our
behaviors. Sinful partying, affairs, personal wrecks and other
disasters come from the influence of alcohol and drugs.

But power for godly, blessed and joyful living comes through
the Holy Spirit, as He ministers the reality of the Resurrection
in our lives!

So if it were possible that Christ died for our sins but didn't
rise again, we might be prepared for Heaven by receiving Him

and His work as our substitute, but we wouldn't have the power to live our lives here on earth.

Many "unbelieving" people believe that Jesus lived. In fact, it's hard to find anybody who doesn't think Jesus is a verifiable historical character. But only to believe that He lived on earth and died, never to rise again, is to lop off half of what it means to be a Christian!

Following Him doesn't only prepare us for dying (through His death on our behalf) but also for living (through His life, which burst out of the tomb).

- If Christ is not risen, then there is no eternal future for us.

Some believe a human is nothing more than a sophisticated machine. A person is just a conglomeration of biochemistry hopping across nerve endings, or synapses. They believe there is no soul or spirit, just a physical body responding and reacting to its environment.

However a person is not merely a behaving animal, but a human being. This reality is rooted in the very nature of God. His name is "I AM." God is eternal Being, and we are His people. That godly being is stolen from us in the fall into sin, but restored when we receive Jesus Christ. He said He is the Zoë—the life—of God. To have God's life is to have being.

But if there is no Resurrection, there is no eternal being. We are born to be religious in our striving to do good, but we have no hope beyond our biological existence in the material world.

Take away the belief and confidence in the Resurrection, and you strip a person of the "living hope"!

- If Christ is not risen, all we have is a religion called "Christianity", not a relationship with a living Lord.

Christ's followers were first called "Christian" by non-believers at Antioch. It wasn't because the people there saw a church building or read a fat theology book. The idol-worshippers at Antioch called Christ's followers "little Christs" because they saw Christ in their lives!

People weren't converted to Christianity, they were led to Christ, and Christ converted them to Himself. If Christ weren't raised from the dead, people would have simply been transferring their Judaism or Greek worship for a new religion— Christianity.

Take away the belief and confidence in the Resurrection, and you strip a person of the living hope!

But Christ was—and is—alive, and Christians with their transformed lives were and are proof of it!

- If Christ is not risen, He's a hoax, not the Savior; but if He is risen from the dead, He is all He said He is.

C.S. Lewis said you can't believe Jesus was a good moral teacher, and not the Son of God. A moral teacher would not lie. Since He claimed to be God's Son, then Jesus is either, in Lewis' words, a liar, lunatic or Lord.

The Resurrection proves more than anything else that Jesus Christ is Lord. That term means He is supreme, that everything must and will bow to Him ultimately, as Paul writes in Philippians.

This is a direct threat to the powers of darkness and their evil leader. After all, it was his great aim to lift his throne above all others. But if Jesus has risen from the dead, then He really is Lord, and the evil one doesn't have a chance!

So, the prince of darkness will pay the bribe with mounting desperation as the end of time and his own judgment approaches.

Chapter 11

God's
Choice Work

Religions, theologies, denominations and individual churches all have their ideas about the nature of God's "work." For some, it's social action, while for others, God's favored "work" is ritual, still others insist the "work" God desires most for His people is evangelism.

There can be no doubt that bringing people to Christ is really important. Touching society with transformation is crucial, as well. "Ritual" might even be seen as vital when churches observe baptism and the Lord's Supper.

But stopping these activities is not the purpose of the bribe.

Jesus defined God's "choice work" when He said, "This is the work of God, that you believe in Him whom He has sent" (John 6:29 NASU).

BELIEF GETS US POSITIONED

Belief positions us for everything else God will do in our lives. Belief is like the cord linking a lamp to the electricity. The Holy Spirit is the power for living, and our lives don't radiate God's glory if we're not "plugged in." But we don't have the Holy Spirit apart from Jesus (Romans 8:9).

Belief positions us for everything else God will do in our lives.

So it all comes back to the central argument of this book: The world, the flesh and the devil do all possible to bribe us to keep us from believing "on" and "in" Jesus and His Resurrection, and we must refuse to accept the bribe.

"Believing" is our core work. If we don't do that, we will be unable to do anything else.

In the preceding chapters, we've detailed some of the ways the "world" tries to bribe us. Sometimes in the New Testament, "world" is the translation of a Greek word meaning "age." Paul writes, "Now we have received, not the spirit of the world, but the Spirit who is from God, so that we may know the things freely given to us by God..." (1 Corinthians 2:12 NASU)

Every "age" is characterized by its own culture, and every culture has its methods for bribing people not to believe in the living Jesus. In some societies, the bribe is paid through the occult. In voodoo cultures, for example, people enter overt covenants with demons to get "good luck," health or prosperity. Obviously, the bribe is a sham because many occultic societies are among the worlds poorest—like Haiti.

In other cultures the bribe may be in the form of rationalism. Several societies in Western Europe have branded Christian belief as an insane cult. There have even been suggestions that evangelism be restricted, as it is in some Asian countries.

Every age is chacterized by its own culture, and every culture has its methods for bribing people not to believe in the living Jesus.

The spirit of the age pays out unimaginable treasure to keep people from believing in Jesus Christ and His Resurrection.

The flesh lusts after the bribe. Whether it's the recognition and applause of a cynical world or the false promise of protection and prosperity held out by the demonic— the flesh desires it.

In fact, people who have heard the Gospel but not believed

find a conflict. There's something in their spirit that wants to believe, but the flesh fights it. And everything in culture rallies on the side of the flesh. Movies, television, resorts, like Las Vegas, and red light districts from Bourbon Street to Amsterdam's rotten "adult" district all try to bribe the flesh.

Buying the souls of people is the devil's passion. If the work of God is to believe, then the devil's work is to doubt. Jesus came to save, but the devil comes only to destroy. To accomplish this disastrous agenda, the enemy will use the world and the flesh in incredibly subtle ways to sweeten the bribe.

CHURCHES GET CAUGHT TOO

Even churches fall into this trap. Earlier I mentioned the dangers of the tax exempt status, but the bribe is more than that. Culture promises to give the church a "place" and a "voice" if only the churches will sing the world's song. Many churches want the recognition, and accept the bribe. The only "voice" the culture accepts is a formal, powerless, Jesus-empty prayer at banquets.

Don't fall for the bribe. It will keep you from the core work of God, which is believing on His Son and His Resurrection. Without that foundation of faith and the confidence and power it brings, everything else is dead works!

Chapter 12

from the **bribe** to the **Bride**

All it takes to defeat the Bribe is for the Church to rise up and be the Church!

This means moving in the reality of Jesus' promise in Matthew 16, where He tells Peter, as a representative and symbol of all the people who will follow Him,

> "I also say to you that you are Peter, and upon this rock I will build My church; and the gates of Hades will not overpower it. I will give you the keys of the kingdom of

heaven; and whatever you bind on earth shall have been bound in heaven, and whatever you loose on earth shall have been loosed in heaven."

—MATTHEW 16:18-19

The Church today must possess the Kingdom of God, walk in its authority, and refuse to buy into the Bribe that has been passed down through the centuries. As we walk in our rightful authority, the Church will impact every segment of society.

So it's time to declare, "No more silence!"

> Jesus is coming back for a Bride, but the church today looks more like a bag lady.

Jesus is coming back for a Bride, but the Church today looks more like a bag lady. Her garments are stained by the lies of the Bribe she has lived on far too long. But as the Church grabs hold of the truth she will get herself ready for the Bridegroom, and her garments will become beautiful again. Not only that, but her life will be charged with new power, and her effectiveness will be so great people everywhere will be drawn to her Bridegroom.

This newly energized Church will be bold enough to expose the cover-up, and pull off the blinders that keep people from understanding what's going on under the table. The enemy's dirty tactics will be revealed, and the truth about God's intended plan for His Church will be seen in all its beauty.

LATTER GREATER THAN FORMER

God's Word is clear about how we should be living in this age and what we ought to be doing. Haggai the Prophet reveals the heart of God when he writes, under the power of the Holy Spirit, "The latter glory of this house will be greater than the former,' says the LORD of hosts, 'and in this place I will give peace,' declares the LORD of hosts" (Haggai 2:9).

Our church—Rock City Church in Baltimore, Maryland—has experienced this prophetic vision in unusual ways. For example, Compassion Commission, one of our ministries, is touching urban areas with the glory of God. CC draws 150 youth from across America for one week every year. They help rebuild an inner city house completely. At the end of the week, there's a huge block party, and the refurbished house is given to a needy family who had never owned a home of their own. Hundreds of lives are touched by the Gospel message, and food and clothing are distributed, along with counseling and prayer.

We've discovered that the Church is the Church in those inner city blocks!

When the Bride of Christ leaves the neighborhood at the

end of the day, the block is cleaner, the people are happier, peace is restored, and dozens have accepted Christ as Savior. [1]

This is an example of the "latter house" working in a way greater than the "former," as stated in Haggai. God said through His prophet that He would give "peace" through the "latter house." We see this in the neighborhoods where the Compassion Commission ministers. "Peace" is the Hebrew word shalom, and it refers not merely to emotional tranquility, but to well-being, including material blessings in every area of life.

There's a description of the composition of this "latter house" in Ephesians 2:19-22, where Paul writes,

> So then you are no longer strangers and aliens, but you are fellow citizens with the saints, and are of God's household, having been built on the foundation of the apostles and prophets, Christ Jesus Himself being the corner stone, in whom the whole building, being fitted together, is growing into a holy temple in the Lord, in whom you also are being built together into a dwelling of God in the Spirit.

Here we see that the Church, wherever it's located, is to be the place of worship, healing, equipping, hearing and receiving God's instructions.

Why isn't the Church like this everywhere?

Somewhere along the way man started preaching the gospel of man and stopped proclaiming the Gospel of the Kingdom. The Bribe had been passed down for so long that it's been accepted as the essence of modern Christianity and the norm for the state of the Church in many places.

To **deny** **the** resurrection of **Jesus** is to **strip** the **church** of **its** **power** as **well** **as** its **glory!**

Remember, to deny the Resurrection of Jesus Christ is to strip the Church of its power as well as its glory!

The gospel of ignorance is at war with the Gospel of knowledge, which is the truth of the Kingdom of God. Ignorance is darkness, but God's Kingdom is light, which illuminates the everlasting revelation with present-day understanding and application.

PASSPORT SURRENDERED

When humanity sinned against God, as a race we lost our citizenship in God's Kingdom. We had to surrender our Kingdom passport—as symbolized in the loss of Eden and its entrance being barred from us. We accepted the passport from the world of compromise—boldly stamped with the word BRIBE.

Then, under Satan's corrupt government, the kingdom of darkness flooded in. The serpent controls his subjects by keeping them in the dark regarding spiritual truth. To do this, Satan blinds people's minds (2 Corinthians 4:4). The destroyer started this the day the Bribe was accepted, and he has raised the stakes continually, requiring more and more payoffs.

But the "latter house" is to be Bribe-free and full of light. This is what Paul writes in Colossians 1:12-14:

For the church to effectively change her communities she must change and clarify her message.

... giving thanks to the Father, who has qualified us to share in the inheritance of the saints in Light. For He rescued us from the domain of darkness, and transferred us to the kingdom of His beloved Son, in whom we have redemption, the forgiveness of sins.

Thus, for the Church to effectively change her communities and nations—and ultimately the world itself—she must change and clarify her message by committing herself to a renewed preaching of the good news of God's Kingdom.

This puts the light on the Bribe of compromise, exposing it for what it is. The more it is revealed in its ugliness, the more the truth will gain the attention of the whole Church, once and for all.

Jesus was open about His intent, and the Church must be clear on her mission and purpose. At the outset of His public ministry, Jesus went to the synagogue in Nazareth, where He was raised, and took the scroll of Isaiah on a Sabbath day. He read words now labeled as being from Isaiah 61. Jesus' reading of this passage and accompanying words are recorded in Luke 4:18-19:

> The Spirit of the Lord is upon me, because he hath anointed me to preach the gospel to the poor; he hath sent me to heal the brokenhearted, to preach deliverance to the captives, and recovering of sight to the blind, to set at liberty them that are bruised, To preach the acceptable year of the Lord.

Jesus states His mission in terms no one could miss: He had come to proclaim the Kingdom of God and do its works. "This day is this scripture fulfilled in your ears", He told the people at the synagogue (Luke 4:21 KJV). They were upset because when Jesus said "The Spirit of the Lord is upon Me," He was

applying the words in Isaiah to Himself. "I am *ho Christos*—the Anointed One," Jesus was telling the crowd.

STILL UPSET

Today people are still upset, but they fall back on the reassuring word that these are the last days, and Jesus will be returning soon. The facts, however, don't support that, especially in light of what Jesus said 2,000 years ago at the Nazareth synagogue, and especially some two years later, when He was walking with His disciples in Jerusalem.

> Jesus primary message was God's rule in the universe, and the authority of His kingdom people.

"This gospel of the kingdom shall be preached in the whole world as a testimony to all the nations, and then the end will come," He said that day (Matthew 24:14).

Of the six billion people on earth, many have yet to hear the basics of the Gospel, let alone the Gospel of the Kingdom. Jesus didn't preach only about being born again, being healed and baptized, but about the Kingdom. Again and again the Gospel writers report that He came to this region or that, "preaching the Kingdom."

Jesus primary message was that of God's rule in the universe, and the authority of His Kingdom people. This wasn't a message about our "heavenly home when we die" (though certainly that's true) or a touchy-feely Kum-Ba-Yah sermonette, but a powerful announcement that the Kingdom of God was at hand.

And it was—and is—because the Kingdom, lost from the earth in the Garden, returns in seed-form in Jesus Himself! The Kingdom is not far off in some distant future, but it's "D-Day" invasion occurred the moment Jesus entered the world.

The Kingdom of God doesn't refer to mere physical territory. It is a jurisdiction in which God's influence has full authority. That means God's Kingdom is my neighborhood because I live there and His Kingdom is in me.

From Abraham all the way to the 400-years of silence known as the Inter-testamental Period when no prophetic word was heard from God, and right up to the emergence of John the Baptist, people understood little about the Kingdom. Then Jesus came, and history took on a new shape:

> "The Law and the Prophets were proclaimed until John; since that time the gospel of the kingdom of God has been preached, and everyone is forcing his way into it"
>
> —LUKE 16:16

Thus, in this day we are merely carrying out the policies of

THE Bride of Great Price •

our King. We are Christ's ambassadors (2 Corinthians 5:20), and as any good ambassador does, we represent the Kingdom of our citizenship in alien territory. We can carry out only the orders of our King, and that's why we must stay close to Him.

And we discover that if we take care of His interests, He takes care of ours. That's Jesus' point in Matthew 6:31-32, when He says,

> "Do not worry then, saying, 'What will we eat?' or, 'What will we drink?' or, 'What will we wear for clothing?' For the Gentiles eagerly seek all these things; for your heavenly Father knows that you need all these things. But seek first His kingdom and His righteousness, and all these things will be added to you. So do not worry about tomorrow; for tomorrow will care for itself. Each day has enough trouble of its own."

Jesus provides everything necessary for us to minister the kingdom within this world.

A real ambassador has all he needs to represent his government and nation, whether it's an office, car, computer, staff or bread on the table. Jesus provides everything necessary for us to minister the Kingdom within this world.

from the **bribe**
to the **Bride**

Perhaps the greatest damage done by the Bribe is blurring that Kingdom focus. The Resurrection of Jesus Christ was the ultimate validation of the Kingdom. Miracles were signs confirming the truth of Christ's message, and the Resurrection was the greatest of all miracles. To deny that is to hide the truth about Jesus and the Kingdom, and that's what the Bribe is all about.

This is the primary reason the Church has strayed from its core message and ministry. The Bribe paid to the soldiers 2,000 years ago was whispered and received across history until the truth about the Resurrection was distorted like those messages people pass from ear to ear around a circle, causing the final report to be nowhere close to the original.

Losing the center means things fall apart, to paraphrase the poet, Yeats. So the Church split, with one group concerning itself with the spiritual life of human beings and the other social action: spiritual versus material, personal salvation versus social transformation, eternal versus temporal, heavenly versus earthly, and sacred versus secular.

This split view has been exaggerated and expanded by an increasing emphasis on the immediate return of Christ, and the concept that everything secular is destined for Hell. Many in the Church embraced the idea that all we can do is get souls saved.

RAPTURE MENTALITY

This is the hurry up "rapture mentality." It hurts our effectiveness, as the present state of the world shows. Never have there been more Christians in more churches speaking more languages throughout the world, yet it would seem that never has the Church had less impact on its culture than right now.

We blame the "pagans" for the secularization of our culture—the loss of the meaning of Christmas, the Sabbath, the celebration of Christ's Resurrection, and other days and seasons that were once regarded as sacred. Yet the real problem is with the Church. She has lost her vision of the instrument by which God confronts and transforms culture.

When we buy into the Bribe, we crawl back into the corner, doing nothing as all mention of God is slowly being removed from public life. The Bribe causes us to see no connection between God and the workplace. Rather than seeing our work as fulfilling the call of God to be an ambassador of Christ on the job, we see it merely as a means to make money.

When this happens, truly, the salt has lost its savor (Matthew 5:13).

The Gospel of salvation, which prepares people for life after death, is foundational. However, the Gospel doesn't stop there because the Gospel of the Kingdom is for life in the here and now. We must not only be prepared to die, but also to live!

The Church will overcome the negative impact of the Bribe only when she thrusts herself into every facet of society—education, politics, the arts and entertainment, finance and business. We must stop preaching the separation from sin as separation from society.

We can live our born-again lives—without compromise—in every part of society. We must change our message from merely being about separation from the world and culture to that of infiltrating and influencing our world and culture.

Jesus never asked that we be taken from the world. In fact, in John 17, as He prays for His disciples across the ages, He prays to the Father,

> "I do not ask You to take them out of the world, but to keep them from the evil one."
> —JOHN 17:15

We need to penetrate society with Christ's life and love, and with a real demonstration of His anointing. If we do this, individually and collectively, we will become the very best at whatever we put our hands to. And that, my brothers and sisters, will greatly glorify God.

Then the lies behind the Bribe will be exposed and dealt with once and for all!

He is Alive!

End Notes

CHAPTER 1

1. "Evidence for the Resurrection," By Josh McDowell. Retrieved from http://www.leaderu.com/everystudent/easter/articles/josh2.html.

CHAPTER 2

1. "Police storm Christian's home," WorldNetDaily, June 23, 2007. Retrieved from http://www.worldnetdaily.com/news/article.asp?ARTICLE_ID=56323.
2. Ibid.
3. Ibid.
4. McDowell, op. cit.
5. Ibid.
6. Ibid.
7. "Poll: More Americans prefer 'Merry Christmas' greeting," CNN.com, December 20, 2005. Retrieved from http://www.cnn.com/2005/US/12/20/poll.season/.
8. "Christmas story film targets schools, Manchester Evening News, October 5, 2005. Retrieved from http://www.manchestereveningnews.co.uk/entertainment/film_and_tv/s/176/176642_christmas_story_film_targets_schools.html.
9. Ibid.
10. "Student sues college for psychiatric abuse," By Jon Doughtery, WorldNetDaily, January 5, 2001.

Retrieved from http://www.worldnetdaily.com/
news/article.asp?ARTICLE_ID=21225.

CHAPTER 3

1. "Jihad and Genocide," By Faith McDonnell,
Touchstone: A Journal of Mere Christanity, 2004.
Retrieved from http://www.touchstonemag.com/
archives/article.php?id=17-06-076-r.

CHAPTER 4

1. "Is God making a difference in Tinsel Town?", By
Phil Cooke, ChristianAnswers.Net. Retrieved from
http://www.christananswers.net/spotlight/movies/
discernment/findinggodinhollywood.html.

2. "China: Will it become a Christian nation?" By Janice
Shaw Crouse, PhD. Retrieved from http://www.
beverlylahayeinstitute.org/articledisplay.asp?id=2084
&department=BLI&categoryid=dotcommentary.

3. Ibid.

4. 'Leading Atheist Philosopher Concludes God's Real,'
Associated Press, December 9, 2004. Retrieved from
http://www.foxnews.com/story/0,2933,141061,00.
html.

5. "Church loses tax exempt status," By Julie Foster,
WorldNetDaily, May 13, 2000. Retrieved from http://
www.freerepublic.com/forum/a391d19af0f3b.htm.

6. "Church, Inc.," By Mark Bergin, World Magazine,
June 9, 2007. Retrieved from http://www.worldmag.
com/articles/13031.

CHAPTER 5

7. "Egyptomania." Retrieved from http://en.wikipedia.
org/wiki/Egyptomania

8. "One Nation Under Gods," By Richard Ostling, Time,
December 2, 1993. Retrieved from http://www.time.
com/time/magazine/article/0,9171,979737,00.html.

CHAPTER 6

1. "Humanist Manifesto II," American Humanist Association. Retrieved from http://www. americanhumanist.org/about/manifesto2.html.

CHAPTER 7

1. This summary of Barton's findings is from "What happens if prayer is banned at school assemblies?" By Rob McCafferty, Port Elizabeth Church Net. Retrieved from http://www.pechurchnet.co.za/post/ issues/education/ed20030429.htm.

CHAPTER 8

1. "Darwin's Black Box," By Dr. Ray Bohlin. Retrieved from http://www.leaderu.com/orgs/probe/docs/ darwinbx.html.

CHAPTER 9

1. "Apostasy In The Church," By David R. Reagan. Retrieved from http://www.lamblion.com/articles/ prophecy/signs/Signs-05.php.
2. "Rediscovering the Historical Jesus," By Dr. William Land Craig. Retrieved from http://www.leaderu.com/ offices/billcraig/docs/rediscover1.html.
3. Retrieved from http://www.bible.org/illus. hp?topic_id=94.
4. Arthur Guiterman, Gaily the Troubadour, New York: E.P. Dutton Co., 1936. Retrieved from ibid.

If you would like information on the Compassion Commission, contact us at Rock City Church, 1607 Cromwell Bridge Road, Baltimore, Maryland 21234.

New Releases

from

GATEKEEPER

BISHOP BART PIERCE

COVER ME
IN THE
DAY OF BATTLE

FILLING TODAY'S NEED
FOR SPIRITUAL COVERING

Order Your Copy Today!

ISBN: 978-0-9776892-1-7 ♦ Paperback ♦ US $13.99

BISHOP BART PIERCE

Fulfilling Today's Need for Spiritual Fathers

Why do good Christian soldiers—pastors, leaders, intercessors, and others—lose some of the battles we all face daily? Is it possible that they fail to reach their greatest potential because they go to battle without the covering of a spiritual father?

In this day of do-it-your-selfism, Bishop Bart Pierce says it's time to address our need for fathers—both spiritual and natural. It's God's desire and the groan of the world for mature sons to come forth.

Fathers, arise now, and raise up sons. Sons, arise, and get your heads covered, and let's go to battle under the covering of God and our fathers. Then the curse of fatherlessness will be broken, and sons will turn to fathers and fathers will turn to sons, so that the Church can be the force God created it to be.

John Louis Muratori

Rich Church

Poor Church

UNLOCK the SECRETS of CREATING WEALTH
and HARNESS the POWER of MONEY
TO INFLUENCE EVERYTHING

#1 Source *for* Financial Wisdom

ISBN-13: 978-0-9704753-1-2 • Hardcover • US $19.95

JOHN LOUIS MURATORI

Finally, a unique and insightful book about the controversial topic of wealth building. This book will clarify the issue like none other—it is truly in a league of its own. John Muratori chronicles the history of both God and prosperity, and Biblical economics.

—— Topics ——

- The History of God & Prosperity
- The Twelve Biblical Laws of Wealth Creation
- Wealth Transference
- A Comprehensive Exposition on the Transference of Wealth from both a Social Economic and Biblical Economic Perspective

- How and Why the Church Has Been Deceived to Eliminate the Message of Wealth and Prosperity
- Unlocking the Wealth Building Secrets of Judaism
- Answering the age old question: Why Do The Wicked Prosper and How it Relates to the Readers Personal Sphere of Influence

- The Superiority of Biblical Wisdom Concerning Wealth and Finance

The priceless insights are guaranteed to move every reader to a fresh level of empowerment and financial liberation.

Written in an informative easy to read style, the emerging generation will quickly grasp this invaluable knowledge. It is a book parents will give to their children to equip them for Biblical prosperity.

Not just a theoretical treatise, but a practical blueprint for financial influence destined to liberate every single reader.

Just the information of the twelve biblical laws of wealth creation would be enough for the reader to be enriched beyond measure.

These principles are trans-generational. It's scriptural message is universal and can be transferred to any culture or country in the world.

The incredible adventure and inestimable wealth of *Rich Church Poor Church* awaits you!

Foreword by A.R. BERNARD

WHO'S YOUR Daddy NOW?

The Cry of a Generation
in Pursuit of Fathers

Doug Stringer

Bestseller!

ISBN: 978-0-9704753-4-3 • Paperback • US $14.95

DOUG STRINGER

Discover *the* AFFIRMATION, ACCEPTANCE *and* APPROVAL *of the* FATHER.

The void created by fatherlessness is a pain that is felt across cultural and generational lines in every area of our society. Whether you grew up with a father in your life, or never felt the love of a father, this is a journey you do not want to miss.

Discover the father's mandate to heal and restore a fatherless generation. Destined to be a classic, Doug has written the book for this hour!

"Doug clearly paints the picture of the role of a father in a child or teen's life and the effects that the absence of fathers are having on this generation. May [these] pages inspire you to aggressively pursue and win your own children's hearts along with the hearts of those who are in need of a spiritual father to mentor and disciple them."

— Ron Luce
President & Founder of Teen Mania Ministries

"Who's Your Daddy Now? will surely resonate strongly with anyone who has ever longed for the love of their natural father as well as anyone who has a heart to be a 'father' to those who need guidance. God has truly equipped Doug in a supernatural way to tear down the walls of this complex subject and to communicate God's truth in a practical yet biblically sound way. This book will be a necessary tool for equipping the Body of Christ and propelling us into a new place in God for generations to come."

— Bishop Eddie L. Long
Senior Pastor, New Birth Missionary Baptist Church

GATEKEEPER PUBLISHING

is expanding its authorship with the launch of our new imprint

'Think Big, Little Books.'

We are looking for fresh, cutting-edge manuscripts that have a relevant message for this hour.

To submit your manuscrip, visit
www.gatekeeperpublishing.com
You can download a manuscript submission form on the "Publishing" page.

Are you a published author trying to make a living writing books?

Consider joining the GateKeeper family of authors. Be a part of a company setting new industry standards. We commit aggressive marketing budgets to every project and give our authors the highest royalties in the trade.

Whatever your situation, GateKeeper can offer you numerous options to suite your specific needs. We offer a full range of services including:

- Complete "book publishing" – from concept to completion

- Innovative Graphics, and full cover design services

- Audio Book Productions

- Foreign Language book production, transcriptions and more

To see our full range of services, or for information on submitting your manuscript, visit our website. You can find our downloadable Manuscript Submission Form on the "Publishing" page.

www.gatekeeperpublishing.com